World Book Myths & Legends Series

NORSE MYTHS & LEGENDS

AS TOLD BY PHILIP ARDAGH

ILLUSTRATED BY STEPHEN MAY

World Book, Inc.
a Scott Fetzer company
Chicago

MYTH OR LEGEND?

Long before people could read or write, stories were passed on by
word of mouth. Every time they were told, they changed a little,
with a new character added here and a twist to the plot there.
From these ever-changing tales, myths and legends were born.

WHAT IS A MYTH?

In early times, people developed stories
to explain local customs and natural
phenomena, including how the world and
humanity developed. These myths were
considered sacred and true. Most include
superhuman beings with special powers.

WHAT IS A LEGEND?

A legend is very much like a myth. The
difference is that a legend is often based on
an event that really happened or a person
who really existed in relatively recent times.

WHO WERE THE NORSE PEOPLE?

The Norse people, who told these stories
around the fireside on cold winter nights,
came from Norway, Sweden, Denmark,
Finland, and Iceland, though they did settle
elsewhere. These were the Viking races—
brave, warrior people living in tough times
in a cruel climate—and most of their myths
and legends were about brave warrior gods.
The earliest versions were being told almost
2,000 years ago, but the stories have changed
a great deal since then.

HOW DO WE KNOW?

Many scenes from myths and legends appear
on Viking carvings, and there are also two main
written sources. These are called the *Poetic Edda*
(or the *Elder Edda*) and the *Prose Edda*. The
Prose Edda is a collection of the most famous
myths and legends, written down by a man
from Iceland called Snorri Sturluson, who
lived from 1179 to 1241.

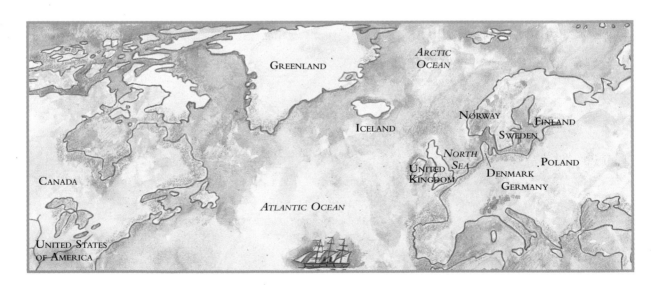

The stories were already very old when he put them on paper, but it's thanks to him that we know so much today. The *Poetic Edda* is a collection of 38 anonymous poems.

THE NORSE WORLD

The Norse people had a very clear picture of what their world looked like. In fact, they saw it as nine different worlds.
ALFHEIM home of the light elves.
VANAHEIM home of the fertility gods.
ASGARD home of the warrior gods called the Aesir, connected by **Bifrost** (a rainbow bridge) to MIDGARD home of the humans.
NIDAVELLIR land of the dwarfs.
JOTUNHEIM land of the giants.
SVARTALFHEIM home of the dark elves.
NIFLHEIM includes Hel, the realm of the dead.
MUSPELL a place of fire.

THE TREE OF LIFE

The nine worlds were held together by the roots of the mighty **Yggdrasil**, a tree growing up into the stars.
Ratatosk, a squirrel, ran up and down the branches, trunk, and roots of Yggdrasil, delivering insults between the birds and the dragon **Nidhogg**. The dragon chewed at the roots, trying to destroy the tree.

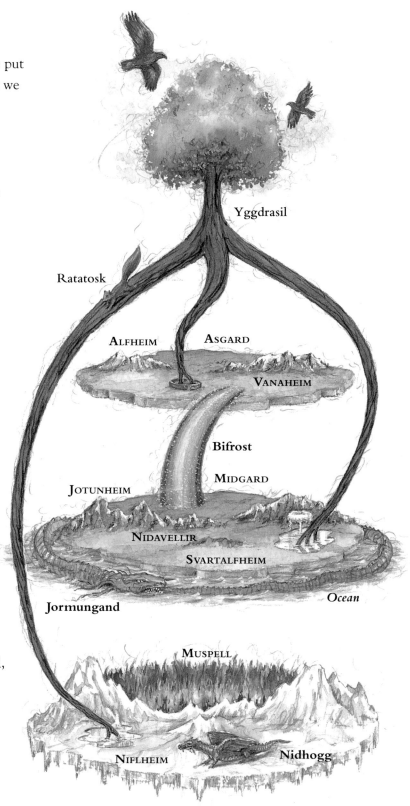

Yggdrasil

Ratatosk

ALFHEIM   ASGARD

VANAHEIM

Bifrost

MIDGARD

JOTUNHEIM

NIDAVELLIR

SVARTALFHEIM

Ocean

Jormungand

MUSPELL

NIFLHEIM   Nidhogg

GODS, GIANTS, & DWARFS

In some myths and legends, the gods are immortal and live forever. That's not so with the Norse gods. They *can* be killed. In fact, Norse myths and legends predict that one day all the gods *will* be killed in a mighty battle against the giants called Ragnarok. Here are some of the characters you will meet in this book. Many have more than one wife or husband. Some of the alternative spellings of their names are in parentheses.

ODIN (Woden) One-eyed chief of all the gods, has a throne, Hlidskialf, and two advisers: the ravens Hugin and Munin. A brave warrior, he is the husband of Frigga and father of many of the gods.

FRIGGA (Frigg) Wife of Odin and mother of most of his children. Her favorite son is the handsome Balder. She is the most powerful goddess in Asgard.

THOR God of thunder. Rides across the skies in a chariot pulled by goats, has the hammer Mjollnir and the belt Meginjardir. Short tempered, but likes humans. A popular god with the Norse people.

TYR God of war. The bravest of all the gods, as well as being honorable and true. Famous for having just one hand. If you want to know how he lost the other one, read "Tyr and the Jaws of Fenris" (page 19).

BALDER (Baldr) God of light. The most handsome of all the gods, and Frigga's favorite son.

HODER (Hod, Hodr) Balder's twin brother, who is blind. The prophecies say that after the mighty battle of Ragnarok he and Balder will be born again.

LOKI Master trickster, half a giant and half a god, friend of Odin and Thor and murderer of Balder. Sometimes very funny, but can be very cruel.

HEL (Hela) Goddess of death, daughter of Loki. The lower half of her body is like a corpse's, with exposed bones and putrid flesh.

FREY (Freyr) God of summer, whose chariot is pulled by a huge wild boar.

FREYA (Freyja) Goddess of beauty, whose chariot is pulled by two large cats.

KVASIR Said to be the wisest of all the gods in Asgard.

HOENIR (Honir) In some stories about the earliest gods, he is said to be Odin's brother. In others, that honor goes to Ve and Vili.

AEGIR (Hler) God of the sea, husband of Ran. Lord of the world beneath the waves where drowned sailors spend their days.

RAN Goddess of the sea, who pulls sailors from their boats in a large net, dragging them under water.

HEIMDALL The god who guards Bifrost, the rainbow bridge joining the home of the gods to the other worlds.

UTGARD-LOKI The giant king of Utgard, in Jotunheim. Very clever and crafty. Once disguised himself as a giant called Skrymir to teach Thor a lesson.

HREIDMAR A dwarfish king with three sons—Otter, Fafnir, and Regin. Held Odin hostage for a huge pile of treasure.

FAFNIR A son of Hreidmar. Killed his father for his treasure, exiled his brother Regin, then turned himself into a dragon.

HYRROKKIN A terrifying giantess who rides an enormous wolf, using writhing vipers as reins.

SKIRNIR A brave and faithful servant to the god Frey.

The Viking era was from about A.D. 700 to 1070. This is a Viking runestone. The carvings are called runes and are the earliest form of Norse writing.

THOR IN THE LAND OF THE GIANTS

A mighty war chariot hurtled across the night sky pulled by two massive goats with burning eyes and vicious, curled horns. Their hoofs cracked the air around them with sparks of lightning and filled the darkness with the sound of thunder. At the reins stood a god with wild hair, a wild beard, and wild eyes: a warrior god. This was Thor, the god of thunder.

Once Thor visited a place called Utgard, in the land of the giants. With him went his friend Loki, who was half a giant and half a god, and two servant children, Thialfi and his sister Roskva.

Around his waist Thor wore Meginjardir, a thick belt that doubled his already superhuman strength. Tucked into it was his gigantic throwing hammer called Mjollnir—a magic hammer that always returned to him once it had struck and killed an enemy. Even a glancing blow from it meant certain death.

When Thor and his band of travelers entered the vast hall of the king of the giants, the giants laughed at him. They called him "small" and "insignificant" and mocked him.

"Silence!" cried Thor, raising his bone-crushing hammer above his head. "Even if I were a simple traveler, I would not expect to be treated in this way. Where is your respect?"

"Respect?" bellowed Utgard-Loki, king of the giants, his voice echoing around the massive hall.

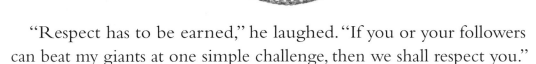

"Respect has to be earned," he laughed. "If you or your followers can beat my giants at one simple challenge, then we shall respect you."

"Very well," replied Thor, his thin-lipped smile hidden by his beard. "We accept." He knew that he could defeat the giants at anything.

Thor's friend Loki pushed his way to the front of the group.

"I challenge anyone to beat me in an eating competition!" he cried. He felt sure that he would win because there was only one thing he enjoyed more than mischief-making, and that was eating.

"An excellent challenge!" boomed the giant king. "Let us prepare."

Soon a massive table was laid with plates of food from end to end. At one end stood Loki. At the other end was a strange-looking giant named Logi, dressed in flaming orange.

On a nod from the giant king, the race began. Both Loki and Logi ate as fast as they could, working their way down the table. When they met in the middle, Loki had eaten every scrap of meat, every vegetable, and every piece of fruit from his half of the table. Who could beat that?

The giant, Logi, that was who—for he had eaten all that and more. He had eaten every bone and even the plates on which the food was served. Thor's group had failed in their first task.

Next Thor's servant boy Thialfi agreed to a race against a boy giant called Hugi across the floor of the vast stone-flagged hall. Thialfi and Hugi lined up, and Thor threw back his head and shouted "GO!"

Thialfi sprang forward with all his might, only to hear the giants cheering as though someone had already reached the far wall. Someone had. To the boy's utter amazement, Hugi had already run the course and was being hoisted on the giants' shoulders in celebration.

Exhausted and defeated, Thialfi returned to his master.

"You did your best," bellowed Thor. "We only have to beat them at one task, and now it is my turn."

He faced the king of the giants, who was leaning back in his huge wooden throne, clearly enjoying events.

"What challenge will you make, little thunder god?" the king asked, a chuckle rising in his throat.

"I challenge you to a drinking match," said Thor, his eyes burning with anger at the way the giants were treating him. "We'll see who can drink the most horns of wine."

"Our wine is very strong," said the king. "Let us see who can drink the most horns of water." He clapped his enormous hands, and a huge drinking horn was brought into the hall. "You start," said the king.

Thor tipped the end of the horn to his lips and drank and drank and drank . . . but, however much he drank, he could never empty the horn. Finally he had to admit defeat.

"If you can't drain even a single horn, there's no competition," shrugged the giant king. "Perhaps you should try something easier, such as lifting my cat from its place by the fire and putting it on my lap."

Thor's face reddened with anger.

"Oh, well, if that's too difficult for you . . . ," the giant teased him.

Thor charged toward the fireplace and the sleeping cat.

"That's strange," Roskva whispered to her brother. "I'm sure that cat wasn't there a moment ago."

Thor reached the cat, bent down, and tried to lift it with one hand . . . then two hands . . . then with both arms. He couldn't lift so much as a single paw off the warm hearth.

Thor couldn't believe what was happening. He was a god, a hero. The people of Midgard stayed up late into the night telling stories of his incredible strength and amazing adventures. What was happening? Ever since he had set foot in Utgard, things had gone terribly wrong.

"I'm tired of your failures," sighed the king of the giants. "Where is the fun in the sport when our two sides are so unevenly matched?"

"Then I offer you one last challenge," said Thor, his deep voice almost a snarl. "I challenge any one of you to a wrestling match. It doesn't matter which of you, the strongest or the tallest—"

"Yes, yes, yes!" said the king with a dismissive wave. "I'll supply you with a worthy opponent. Elli?"

From behind the chief's chair came an old woman—not a giant, just an ordinary-looking old woman, with a bent back and wrinkled skin.

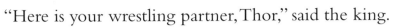

"Here is your wrestling partner, Thor," said the king.

"You expect me to wrestle against her?" gasped Thor.

"You talk of respect but show none," the giant responded with a flash of anger. "This is my old nursemaid. She brought me up as if I were her own son. She is worthy of anything."

"Very well," said Thor, stepping into the center of the hall with the old woman, circled by a ring of spectators.

"There's something wrong," whispered Roskva. "I'm sure that nothing is as it seems."

"Let the wrestling match begin!" cried Loki.

Despite her age Elli was extremely strong. At first Thor was clearly in control, wrestling her this way and that . . . but after much puffing and grunting, the old woman had him down on one knee.

"Enough!" the giant king yelled. "This is no contest. My old nursemaid wins!"

Thor felt humbled. Time and again he and his group had been beaten. He was ashamed. They hadn't won a single challenge and were not worthy of the respect of the giants. The king led them to the gates of his kingdom.

"Now you are leaving, I can tell you the truth of what happened," said the king. "The opponent Loki faced in the eating competition was really Fire, and nothing has a hunger like fire, which eats everything in its path." Loki gasped in amazement.

"As for Hugi, Thialfi's opponent in the race, he was no boy giant but Thought itself, and nothing is faster than a thought. Not even the world's fastest runner could have beaten him."

Thialfi's eyes opened wide in wonder.

"And as for the drinking horn, the other end was in the ocean, which was why you could never empty it," said the giant king. "But you drank so much, Thor, you created the coming in and the going out of the sea." Which is why we now have tides.

"What about the cat?" demanded Roskva.

"The harmless cat that Thor could not lift was Loki's son, Jormungand, magically transformed," the king confessed.

"He is the giant serpent who circles the whole earth, so it was not surprising that Thor couldn't lift him."

"And Elli, your old nursemaid?" asked Thor.

"Old Age herself," said the king, "and old age defeats us all in the end."

Thor felt a fool. "Why did you do this to us?" he asked, in a smaller, quieter voice than he had ever used before.

"Because on your way to Utgard—on the night you slept in a giant's discarded glove, believing it to be a stable—you showed disrespect to a sleeping giant, striking him with your hammer to stop his snoring," the king reminded him. "I was that giant, and I would be dead from the mighty blow of Mjollnir if I hadn't been protected by magic. Now leave my kingdom and never return."

So Thor left with Loki, Thialfi, and Roskva, proud at how well they had competed against Fire, Thought, the Ocean, Jormungand, and Old Age, but also knowing that he been taught a valuable lesson.

Thor went on to many victories and still travels in his chariot across the skies, creating storms wherever he goes. He is remembered and honored, and gives his name to Thursday, which means Thor's day . . . but now he has greater respect for the giants, who are ruled by a very wise and cunning king.

12

THE CURSE OF ANDVARI'S RING

This is a story that spans many generations. It begins with three gods disguised as ordinary human beings, and with an otter that isn't an otter at all. It ends with a young hero and a dragon that was once a dwarf. What brings all these strange people and creatures together? A hoard of gold and a cursed ring.

ONE DAY ODIN, chief of the gods, and his brother Hoenir were walking along a riverbank with Loki. They stopped to watch an otter skillfully catch a salmon in the water.

"That animal is a fine hunter," said Hoenir, "and it has caught a fine fish."

"And made me realize just how hungry I am," said Odin.

"Then let the hunter become the hunted!" cried Loki, throwing a stone at the otter and killing it with a single blow. Odin made a fire, and while Hoenir cooked the huge salmon that had been trapped between its paws, Loki skinned the otter.

Just then a dwarf appeared. He was obviously angry about something because he was ranting and raving so much that none of them could understand a word he was saying. Then he started to gnash his teeth and jump up and down in an absolute fury.

"Calm down, little man," said Odin, putting a friendly hand on the dwarf's shoulder.

This seemed to make the dwarf even angrier.

"Little man?" he spluttered. "*Little man?* I am King Hreidmar!"

"Will you join us in our meal, your majesty?" asked Hoenir.

"I do not eat with murderers!" snapped the dwarfish king.

Loki leaped up, the knife he'd used to skin the otter glinting in the sunlight, but Odin held him back.

"Be careful who you call a murderer," said Odin quietly. "Do you know who I am?"

"You could be the chief of the gods for all I care," cried Hreidmar. "You are still murderers. I sent one of my sons to catch that fish for my dinner table. Like me, he's a shapeshifter. . . ."

". . . and he changed himself into an otter?" asked Hoenir, realizing with horror what had happened. Loki had killed and skinned a dwarfish prince!

Just then two other dwarfs appeared, brandishing weapons. These were Hreidmar's other two sons, Fafnir and Regin. Their weapons were magical and could do the gods serious harm.

"The three of you will be put to death for what you've done!" cried the king.

"Wait," said Odin. "Your son's death was a terrible mistake. Isn't there some way we can repay you for this dreadful accident?"

Hreidmar's eyes lit up at the mention of the word *repay*. He thought for a moment, then said: "I shall let you live if you can stuff the otter's skin with gold and then bury it upright in a pile of treasure, high enough to cover it from nose to tail!"

"We shall gladly do this," said Odin, and as he spoke, he noticed the otter's skin growing bigger and bigger and bigger. There was dwarfish magic in the air, and it would take an enormous amount of treasure to fulfill the bargain.

Leaving Odin and Hoenir as hostages, Loki went off in search of gold. Soon he reached a bend in the river and came upon a waterfall . . . and another dwarf. Loki recognized him as King Andvari, who was reputed to have a hoard of fabulous treasure hidden away somewhere.

As luck would have it, Andvari dived off the bank and turned into a beautiful gleaming trout before he hit the water.

As quick as a flash, Loki pulled out a net borrowed from the goddess Ran—the net she used to pull drowning sailors to their watery graves beneath the waves—and threw it into the water, catching the furious Andvari in its mesh.

"Let me out!" screamed Andvari, who'd already turned himself back into his usual dwarfish form.

No matter how hard he struggled, he couldn't free himself from the goddess's net. Finally he agreed to give Loki a sack of his gold in return for his freedom. The dwarf then took Loki to the place where his gold was hidden. There was so much of it that Loki and Andvari were both bathed in a golden light.

When Loki saw the dwarf's fabulous treasure, he wasn't satisfied with just a sackful. He wanted it all . . . every last piece, down to the ring around Andvari's arm.

"I wouldn't take that if I were you," said the dwarf.

"But you're not me . . . and I choose to have it!" grinned Loki.

"It will bring bad luck, I warn you," said Andvari, who was feeling very sick at the thought of losing all his gold. But Loki snatched the ring and kept it for himself—unaware that the cunning dwarf had laid a curse on it before passing it over.

Using all his strength and skill, Loki made his way back to Hreidmar with the treasure. Odin and Hoenir were pleased at Loki's return, but Hreidmar was happiest of all. Perhaps it was the sight of all that gold that made him smile from ear to ear.

Loki set about stuffing the huge otter's skin and burying it upright, from head to tail, in Andvari's gold.

Soon it was done, and Hreidmar was jumping up and down with glee in a most unkinglike manner.

He was just about to release Odin and Hoenir when he spotted something amiss.

"Wait!" he cried.

"What is it?" asked Loki, who was sure that he had kept his part of the bargain.

"The agreement was that you cover the whole otter with gold," said Hreidmar, a wicked smile spreading across his face.

"And I have," said Loki.

"Then what is this?" demanded the dwarfish king, pointing to the pile of treasure.

Loki peered closely at the pile and could just make out the tip of a single otter's whisker sticking out to one side.

"I have just the thing to cover that," he said, hurriedly placing Andvari's cursed ring over the whisker.

So Odin, Hoenir, and Loki were free to go and went on their way.

The story didn't end there, however, for King Hreidmar and his remaining sons. The curse of the ring was already weaving its evil magic. It started by working its way into Fafnir's mind, making him jealous of his father's new-found wealth.

Soon he wanted the gold for himself—so badly that, one night, he murdered Hreidmar while he lay sleeping.

"Now the gold is mine!" Fafnir whispered into the darkness. "I shall share it with no one."

Just then Regin appeared, yawning.

"What is it, brother?" he asked. Then he noticed his father lying dead at Fafnir's feet and a mad look in Fafnir's eye. He turned and fled, never to return to the land of the dwarfs.

With Regin gone, Fafnir still worried about the safety of his treasure. What if Loki came back, or someone else learned the whereabouts of these untold riches? He would have to guard the hoard forever. So Fafnir turned himself into a dragon and settled down on top of the huge pile of gold.

Time passed, and in exile among humans his brother Regin taught people many dwarfish tricks and ways of life. He showed people how to fashion metals to make tools and weapons, how to harness an ox to a plow, and how to build houses.

Regin had a son who grew to be a strong and handsome. His name was Sigurd. He learned the story of his evil uncle, Fafnir, who had caused his father to live away from his own kind, and traveled to the land of the dwarfs to track him down.

On his journey Sigurd met a stranger who gave him a very important piece of information. He told the young hero that Fafnir, in the form of a scaly dragon, sat day and night on top of his treasure and guarded it with such ferocity that no one could hope to get close enough to harm him. The only time the dragon left the treasure and dropped his guard was when he went to drink from the river.

With this important knowledge about the dragon, Sigurd dug himself a trench near the river and crouched out of sight in it. When Fafnir, in his dragon form, grew thirsty, he slithered off the golden hoard and made his way down to the water—his scaly body passing over the trench where Sigurd waited.

Sigurd grasped his sword and with all his strength plunged the blade into his wicked uncle's breast, tearing it open and killing him.

The exile of Sigurd's father and the death of his grandfather, King Hreidmar, had been avenged . . . and the curse of Andvari's ring had claimed yet another victim.

Tyr and the Jaws of Fenris

A long, long time ago, before most of these tales were even in the minds of those who could see far into the future, the mischievous Loki—half a god and half a giant—secretly married the terrifying giantess Angurboda. They had three children: a writhing serpent, a hideous goddess who was half living, half corpse, and a huge wolf.

L OKI TRIED TO keep his three children a secret, hiding them away. He was well aware that Odin, the one-eyed chief of all the gods, could see everything from his throne.

What Odin saw troubled him greatly. He was horrified by Loki's brood and how big and powerful each was becoming. It seemed likely that they would grow up to be a threat to the gods themselves.

Odin tracked down Loki and his children to a cave, burst in, and grabbed the serpent, spinning it around his head until it flew from his grasp and landed in the ocean. There it grew large enough to circle the whole earth and bite its own tail. This was Jormungand, the giant serpent who lives there still.

As for the hideous rotting goddess, Odin threw her down into Niflheim where she became ruler of the dead and that place that now bears her name—Hel. Here she feeds off the bones of those who do not die honorably in battle.

This left the third child, the wolf called Fenris.

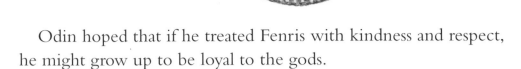

Odin hoped that if he treated Fenris with kindness and respect, he might grow up to be loyal to the gods.

He took Fenris back to Asgard, where he was troubled to find that most of his fellow gods and goddesses were already more than a little afraid of the beast, although he was still a cub.

There was only one god who didn't seem at all frightened of this massive wolf, and that was Tyr, the god of war. It was he who fed Fenris daily. He knew no fear and was kind to the extraordinary creature.

As the wolf grew larger and larger, Odin called a council of gods and goddesses to decide what should be done.

"According to the prophecies, this will be the creature that destroys you, Odin," said one. "I say we kill him before this can happen."

"Prophecies cannot be altered," another protested.

"We cannot slay Fenris, for it was you who brought him here to Asgard and that would be wrong," said Tyr to Odin.

"I agree," said the chief of all the gods. "So what is to be done?"

They finally decided that Fenris needed to be held in place with a large chain so that he couldn't roam free and do any harm. No ordinary chain would do, so they found one famous for its strength, called Laeding.

The problem was how to bind Fenris with it. He would never allow them simply to tie him up. So they suggested to the wolf that this was a game.

"You know we're proud of how strong we are," said one of the gods. "Here's a chance for you to show off your strength. We will bind you in this chain and see how long it takes you to break free."

Unaware that this was a special chain, Fenris agreed and was bound up in Laeding. In next to no time, the enormous wolf was free. He simply tensed his muscles and burst every link of the chain —a shower of twisted pieces of metal fell to the ground.

Pretending to be delighted at how he had proved his incredible strength, the gods praised Fenris, then slunk off, muttering to one another at their failure.

Next they came back with an even stronger chain, known as Dromi, and they used the same trick as before to tie up Fenris.

It seemed only a moment before the chain burst and the huge wolf was free once more.

It was then that the gods realized something that should have occurred to them from the very beginning. Only the most extraordinary binding would be able to hold Fenris. This beast was the son of a giantess and of Loki, who was half a god and also half a giant.

Odin sent for Skirnir, the faithful servant of Frey, god of summer.

"I need you to go quickly to the land of the dwarfs and to visit the underground caves of the finest craftsmen," he said. "Ask them to make the strongest rope or chain, bound together with the strongest magic."

"And what do I offer them in return, sir?" asked the servant, only too well aware of the importance of his visit to the land of the dwarfs, and of the dwarfs' love of gold.

"Tell them that it is to bind Fenris, and they'll accept no payment. They'll know how vital this is to me," said Odin, his single eye fixed firmly on Skirnir. "Do you understand?"

"I understand," nodded Skirnir, and he was off.

Once Skirnir reached the land of the dwarfs, he asked their finest craftsman to create a magical rope that no one—however strong —would be able to break.

"To do this, I need the strongest magic, including five most special ingredients," said the dwarf, whose name is a secret to this day. "I need the sound of the cat's footfall, the beards of women, the mountain's root, the fish's voice, and the bird's spittle."

Now those of you who are thinking that cats' footfalls are silent, that women don't have beards, that mountains don't have roots, and neither do fish have voices, nor birds have spittle are right.

It was because the dwarfs took all these ingredients away from the world of humans long, long ago to fashion the rope Gleipnir, that not one of these things exists any more.

When Skirnir returned to Asgard with the rope, some of the gods were unimpressed. Gleipnir was as smooth and soft as a ribbon made of silk. How could this hold Fenris?

But Odin trusted the magic and took it to the wolf.

"Let us bind you a third time and see if you can escape," he said. Fenris eyed the ribbonlike rope with suspicion.

"No," he said, at last.

"No?" gasped Odin. "Why not?"

"Because if it is an ordinary rope, as it appears, there's no pride in my being able to break free from it," said Fenris.

"If, on the other hand, it is a magic rope, woven from trickery, then I may not be able to escape from it . . . and why should I willingly walk into such a trap?"

Now Odin wasn't going to lie and deny that this was a trap, for that was exactly what it was intended to be.

"Listen," he said. "If you can't break free from this simple ribbonlike rope, you'll pose no threat to us, so of course we shall set you free."

"That may be true," said Fenris, "but I notice that you are careful not to say *when* you'll set me free."

He went on: "I shall play this game, but with one rule of my own. Let one of you put his hand in my mouth while I am tied up with this rope. That way we'll both prove each other's trust. I will trust you not to use trickery and to set me free if I fail. You will trust me not to bite unless . . ." Fenris paused, and ran his drooling tongue across his dagger-sharp teeth, ". . . unless you betray me."

There was silence. Odin looked from one god to another to another, waiting for one to take up the challenge.

Tyr stepped forward while the others looked on, some clutching the remains of the far-thicker chains from which Fenris had so easily freed himself. He thrust his hand between the jaws of the animal he had looked after since the day he had arrived as a pup in Asgard.

Then the gods tied Fenris in the ribbonlike bonds of the magical Gleipnir.

The harder the huge wolf struggled to free himself, the tighter the bonds became, until he could barely move at all.

Perhaps it was because he was tensing his jaw muscles when trying to use every ounce of his strength to free himself, or perhaps it was because he felt betrayed by the one god who had shown him kindness; either way, Fenris snapped his jaws shut, biting off Tyr's hand.

The wolf then opened his mouth wide and howled with such rage that one of the gods thrust a sword between his jaws to wedge them open.

And that is how Fenris came to be tied in place, his jaws wedged open wide. From his mouth poured saliva, which became the foaming torrents of a river. There the tormented animal will remain until the final battle of Ragnarok at the end of time, when he will be able to take revenge on those who trapped him.

And that is also how Tyr, the god of war, comes to have one hand. Some say that this is a sign that a true warrior can take only one side in battle. Some say it is sign that a sword only needs one blade. But many believe that it is a mark that Tyr proved himself to be a brave and loyal god who helped the other gods in a difficult task but was also true to Fenris, one of the three dreadful children of the mischievous Loki.

THE GOD WHO LOVED A GIANTESS

Odin, the chief of all the gods, has a magnificent throne carved from one giant tree. So important and powerful is this seat that it has a special name, Hlidskialf, and only Odin and his wife may sit on it. From this magical throne they see everything that happens in all the nine worlds. . . .

ONE DAY Frey, the god of summer, found the throne empty. Odin was away on one of his fantastic adventures, and there were no other gods about. Frey couldn't resist climbing up onto Hlidskialf's seat . . . just to see what it was like to sit there.

No sooner had Frey sat down than his eyes fell on a beautiful light pulsating in the distance. It hypnotized him. Then the light took on another form, with arms and legs and flowing hair of such radiant beauty that Frey was stunned. This was the magical figure of Gerda, a frost giantess. Frey fell instantly in love.

Now nothing else mattered to Frey. He couldn't sleep or eat. All he could think about was the frost giantess.

But how could he make her love him in return?

He didn't dare tell the other gods what he was feeling because then they'd know that he had sat on Odin's throne. But his faithful servant Skirnir soon discovered his secret.

"I want you to travel to the land of the giants and convince Gerda that I love her and want to marry her," said Frey.

Skirnir was well aware of the dangers of his quest and how unlikely he was to succeed. In return, he asked to be given Frey's magic sword, which could fly through the air and attack an enemy the moment it was drawn from its scabbard. He also borrowed Frey's magnificent horse, Blodughofi, who was afraid of nothing.

Frey gave them willingly. He also handed Skirnir 11 golden apples that would keep Gerda young forever if she ate them. Then he gave him an arm ring to present to the giantess. But this was no ordinary ring—it was Draupnir, Odin's magic ring. Skirnir didn't dare ask how Frey came to have it.

So Skirnir began his quest. It took him a day and a night to ride to the land of the giants, through forests and mountains. He stopped only once, to pick up a magical wooden staff he had found lying in his path.

At his journey's end an enormous hall loomed before him, surrounded by the red flames of an enchantress, protecting it from unwelcome visitors. On either side of the entrance were the biggest and most ferocious hounds Skirnir had ever seen.

But Frey's horse was not afraid of the flames or of the dogs and carried Skirnir past them into the palace. He told the giantess of his quest and of Frey's love for her.

She was unimpressed by the proposal of marriage.

Skirnir offered her the magic golden apples.

"Why should I wish to stay young forever, while those I love grow old around me?" she asked.

He offered her the arm ring of the chief of all the gods himself.

"What use is that to me?" she asked. "Odin may be mighty to gods and humans, but he'd make a very small giant. How could I hope to fit such a ring on even my smallest finger?"

Skirnir did not give up easily. He pointed to Frey's sword.

"This is Frey's magic sword," he said. "If I pull it from its scabbard, it will fly up to your neck and chop off your head."

Gerda laughed. "What good will that do? Frey will still be without a bride, and my father will rip you to pieces, starting with your arms."

Reluctantly Skirnir resorted to his last hope—a terrible curse. He pulled out the wooden staff he had found on his journey there.

"If you will not marry Frey, I shall lay a curse on you," he shouted, his voice echoing around the vast room. "A curse that will make you hungry all the time, but make everything you eat taste like salt . . . a curse that will leave you standing by the entrance to the world of the dead, watching others in torment . . . a curse that will make you an ugly hag. . . ."

"Enough!" cried Gerda. "This Frey you talk of must want to marry me badly. Tell him that I shall be his wife," she sighed. "I will come to him after nine days and nights. Now, go."

Skirnir returned to Frey in triumph.

"What news?" cried the god of summer, stumbling forward to meet him, with a heavy heart and a sense of almost certain failure —for he could see that his servant was traveling alone.

"Gerda has agreed to be your bride," said Skirnir, "but you must wait nine days and nine nights until she comes to you."

Though delighted by Skirnir's news, the next nine days and nights were a torment to Frey. They were like the nine months of winter— cold and dark and seemingly never-ending.

Then, at last, the day came when Gerda left the great hall of her father, Gymir, and went to Frey, meeting him for the very first time . . . and the impossible happened. When the frost giantess stared into the eyes of the love-sick god, she, in turn, fell in love with him.

"Frey," she said, her voice cracking like a hard frost underfoot, "I forgive you your bribes and threats. Let us be together always."

And they still are together, and will be until Ragnarok, the final battle at the end of time. Gerda's magical beauty can be seen today in the aurora borealis, or northern lights, which are strange, moving lights in the skies above the North Pole.

28

THOR'S STOLEN HAMMER

Only someone very foolish or very brave would dare to steal Thor's hammer, Mjollnir, but that's exactly what happened. The story of how Thor and Loki got it back is very funny in places, but the ending is no laughing matter.

One morning Thor woke up with a terrible headache and sat up, rubbing his eyes. He knew that something was wrong before he reached for his magic hammer in his belt, and found it missing. He had sensed that Mjollnir wasn't at his side.

Roaring with rage, he called to his friend Loki, who was asleep by the fire. If anyone had taken Mjollnir as a foolish prank, it would be Loki. But Loki protested that he knew nothing about the whereabouts of the hammer. So where had it gone?

Thor paced up and down the hall, the sound of his footsteps thundering through the skies. When he was angry, the people of Midgard soon knew about it as bolts of lightning crashed around their ears.

"Perhaps you dropped it somewhere?" Loki suggested.

"WHAT?" roared Thor.

"It was only a suggestion," said Loki, but he had to admit that it was a foolish one. There was probably only one thing Thor loved more than his hammer and that was his wife, the goddess Sif.

"Someone has stolen it!" cried Thor, his face so red with anger that it almost matched his beard. "You must help me find it!"

Loki didn't wait to be asked twice. When Thor was angry, it was best to do as he suggested.

Loki decided that he needed to find the quickest way of searching for Mjollnir. One way would be to sit on Odin's throne and see the whole world at once, but he wasn't so foolish as to risk that.

Then he thought of asking to borrow Frey's amazing longboat, which could travel through the skies. It was large enough to hold all the gods and goddesses at once, but when folded up was small enough to fit in your pocket. Loki decided against this because the thief might see the shadow the longboat cast on the ground below and hide Mjollnir.

Loki needed a quick way of traveling across the nine worlds without being recognized or attracting attention. Then he had an excellent idea. He approached Freya, the goddess of beauty. She had a giant falcon's coat, which she often wore to fly around in disguise. This was just what Loki needed and—because of the importance of his task—Freya agreed to lend it to him.

After a while Loki heard stories in the wind that a giant called Thrym had stolen Mjollnir and buried it deep in the earth where no one would find it. Loki asked around and discovered that Thrym was no warrior giant, but a rather ordinary fellow who was head over heals in love with Freya. In fact, Thrym would only reveal Mjollnir's hiding place if the beautiful goddess agreed to marry him.

When Loki told Thor what he had discovered, Thor was delighted. The solution was simple: Freya must become Thrym's bride so that he could have his trusty weapon back. Thor and Loki went to Freya.

"You know how important Mjollnir is—not only to me, but also to all the gods," Thor reminded her. "This mighty weapon has protected the honor of Asgard on many an occasion."

"I am aware of that," Freya nodded, with a suspicious expression on her beautiful face, for she knew that Thor was leading up to something. "That was why I was willing to lend your mischievous friend my magic falcon's coat. Do you think I would have lent it otherwise?"

"Indeed not," said Thor, solemnly.

"I'm happy to report that we now know who has my hammer and why," he went on. "It is a giant called Thrym—"

"Who is a nice enough fellow, as giants go," Loki added, eyeing the necklace around the goddess of beauty's neck. He had once tried to steal it, but had failed.

"A splendid fellow, in fact," Thor agreed. "As a giant of wisdom and one who appreciates great beauty, Thrym wishes to marry you, Freya."

"Which we both think is an excellent idea," Loki added helpfully.

Freya looked from Thor to Loki, then back to Thor.

"You wish me to marry the giant who has stolen Mjollnir?" she asked. Thor nodded.

"And if I marry him, he'll give you back the hammer?" she went on. Thor nodded again.

"So it doesn't matter to you if this Thrym is a dragon, the ugliest of dwarfs, or a sniveling coward. What matters to you is that if I marry him, you'll have your precious hammer back?"

"Well . . . ," began Thor.

"Well . . . ," spluttered Loki.

Freya exploded with rage. She was so angry that even Thor, the great god of thunder himself, was shaken to his bones by her fury. Thor thanked Freya for the use of the falcon's coat; then he and Loki left the goddess with greater haste than their pride would have liked.

Thor and Loki decided that they'd have to trick Thrym into giving Thor his hammer back. But the question was how.

It was Heimdall who came up with the solution. Heimdall was the god whose duty it was to guard Bifrost, the rainbow bridge that connects Asgard, the land of the gods, to the other worlds.

Now Heimdall and Thor didn't see each other often because Thor wasn't allowed to cross the Bifrost. His footsteps were too thunderous and his goat-pulled chariot too wild to cross the rainbow without damaging it. He had to come and go by a different route.

Loki and Heimdall, on the other hand, knew each other only too well. It was Heimdall who had caught Loki trying to steal Freya's necklace, and the two were still enemies. The prophecies said that in the battle at the end of the world, Loki and Heimdall would kill each other.

Heimdall suggested that Thor should dress up as Freya and that Loki should dress as a handmaiden, a woman servant, traveling with her. Thor grumbled into his beard at the idea but, when he couldn't come up with a better one of his own, finally agreed to try it. In their unlikely disguises Thor and Loki went to visit Thrym in his giant hall.

There must have been strong magic at work that night, for despite his booming voice, his hard muscles, and red beard, Thor was mistaken for the beautiful Freya by the giant Thrym—who was so delighted when she arrived that he held a wedding banquet to celebrate.

At the banquet Thrym was shocked by the appetite of his wife-to-be. Thor forgot that he was supposed to be a goddess. He ate a whole ox and a huge platter of salmon and drank two barrels of ale.

Loki had to act fast before their host became suspicious. He quickly explained that Freya had been so excited about meeting and marrying Thrym that she hadn't been able to eat a thing for days.

"Now that you are together at last, she's making up for it," he added.

But things soon turned from bad to worse. Thrym tried to kiss Thor. Not surprisingly, Thor gave him a terrible glare.

"What have I done to offend you, my beautiful one?" Thrym asked. For a moment he suspected that things were not quite as they should be.

Thor was so busy trying to keep himself from tearing Thrym to pieces before he revealed where he'd hidden the hammer, that he was speechless.

Once again quick-witted Loki had to come to the rescue.

"No doubt you've noticed that burning look in my mistress's eyes," he said. Thrym nodded.

"Well, that is a look few men or giants ever live to see. That is the look of a goddess truly in love with burning passion. . . ," Loki added quickly. "Freya is simply thrilled to be so near you."

Loki's words had the desired effect. Delighted by what he'd heard, Thrym got to his feet and called for silence.

"Giants and giantesses," he said grandly, "I am the happiest being in the nine worlds on this day. I love this goddess, Freya." He nodded his huge head in the direction of Thor, who was biting his tongue to keep himself from saying anything. "And she, in her turn, loves me."

The wedding party cheered, and it was then that Thrym made his mistake. . . . He produced Thor's hammer from its hiding place to impress his future bride. Before the giant knew what was happening, he felt Mjollnir snatched from his grasp by the "goddess" who had been his bride-to-be only moments before. But this was no goddess! How could he have been so blind!

Thrym stared in horror at the flaming red beard, the huge muscular body, and the eyes burning with rage. It was Thor himself!

This must have been the thieving giant's last thought before Thor brought his mighty hammer down on Thrym and the other guests in the hall.

Since then Mjollnir has stayed in the hands of Thor, its rightful owner, to be used to defend the honor of the gods and to strike whenever Thor's raging temper gets the better of him.

THE TRICK THAT KILLED A GOD

Balder was the most handsome of the gods. His hair gleamed like sunlight, and he brought goodness, happiness, and wisdom wherever he went . . . until he began to suffer from nightmares and the fear of death.

ODIN AND FRIGGA had many children, but Balder was Frigga's favorite. Balder had a twin brother called Hoder, who was blind, and, sadly, Frigga loved him least of all.

When Frigga learned of Balder's nightmares and fears of death, she decided to do all she could to protect him from harm. She went around the world making every animal, plant, stone, body of water, and illness promise not to harm Balder.

She spoke to the birds in the air, the insects, the leaves on the trees . . . and such was her power as the wife of the mighty Odin that they all promised not to so much as scratch her favorite son.

All, that is, except for one sprig of mistletoe that Frigga passed on her way home. Exhausted after her travels, Frigga glanced at the tiny plant and wondered what harm a small sprig of mistletoe could do to a god. Deciding that the answer was none at all, she did not stop to extract a promise from it.

The news soon spread that Balder was indestructible—that nothing would bruise or scratch him, let alone kill him. And it soon became a regular pastime for the other gods of Asgard to throw things at him in the place called Gladsheim.

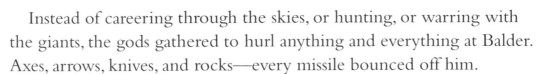

Instead of careering through the skies, or hunting, or warring with the giants, the gods gathered to hurl anything and everything at Balder. Axes, arrows, knives, and rocks—every missile bounced off him.

The gods chose to do this at Gladsheim because it was a place of peace. This showed that the weapons were thrown in jest, not seriousness. Soon Balder was even more popular, and he stopped having nightmares.

Every time a missile was thrown and bounced off him, Balder tossed back his head and laughed at the shared fun of it all.

Once Thor came to Gladshiem with an enormous rock that was so large he barely had the strength to lift it—and he is the strongest god of all. He stepped forward and, with a cry, dropped the rock on Balder's head.

It should have squashed him flat. Instead the rock kept the promise it had made to Frigga and simply rolled off him and fell to the ground with a terrifying crash. Thor threw back his head and joined in Balder's laughter. This was great sport indeed!

Now, if it were possible, Balder looked even more handsome than he had before.

Thor's mischievous friend Loki did not share in the fun. He was used to being the center of attention and was jealous of Balder . . . so he plotted Balder's downfall.

"But how can I fight someone who is indestructible?" he asked himself thoughtfully.

If anyone knew the answer to that, it would be Frigga.

Loki disguised himself as an old woman and went to visit the goddess. Frigga didn't see through Loki's trickery and welcomed him.

When Loki asked about Balder and how nothing seemed to injure him, Frigga was happy to talk about her favorite son. She told the stranger how she had traveled to all corners of the world to extract the promise that nothing would harm him.

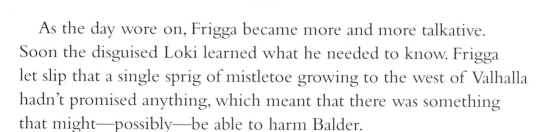

As the day wore on, Frigga became more and more talkative. Soon the disguised Loki learned what he needed to know. Frigga let slip that a single sprig of mistletoe growing to the west of Valhalla hadn't promised anything, which meant that there was something that might—possibly—be able to harm Balder.

"But how could a sprig of mistletoe do that?" she laughed.

"How indeed?" said Loki.

Loki went in search of the sprig of mistletoe. When he found it, he realized that it must have grown since Frigga had seen it. It was now long enough to make a useful weapon.

Loki quickly stripped off the berries and leaves and was left with a thin, straight stem, which he sharpened to a point. He then returned to the gods, who were having a great time throwing things at Balder. They never tired of it. It was such fun watching even the heaviest of rocks or the sharpest of axes bounce off him. What could they throw next?

That day Thor threw his mighty hammer, Mjollnir, at Balder. This was a weapon feared by all. No one hit by it had survived. There were tales of a sleeping giant called Skrymir once being struck with Mjollnir and thinking that the gentle taps were no more than falling leaves—but magic had been at work. Skrymir was, in reality, the giant king Utgard-Loki, and the dents intended for his head were deep enough to create valleys in the invisible hills that stood between his head and the hammer's blows.

Mjollnir simply bounced off Balder and fell to the ground, and the audience of gods cheered and joined in the laughter. Among them sat Balder's blind twin brother, Hoder. Although he could enjoy the conversation and laughter of the other gods, he couldn't join in the fun because he couldn't watch everything bounce off his brother. Loki pushed his way through the throng of gods and handed the seated Hoder the pointed stick of mistletoe.

"Here, Hoder," he said. "You may not be able to see the result, but you can at least take a shot like everyone else. Use my arm to guide you, and you can throw this stick at Balder."

"Thank you, Loki," said Hoder.

Thinking he was simply taking part in the harmless game, Hoder let Loki guide his arm. Hoder threw the mistletoe arrow.

Because the mistletoe had not given the promise made by every other thing in the worlds, the arrow didn't bounce off Balder. The pointed tip tore through his clothes, pierced his heart, and killed him.

There was a shocked silence, followed by the thud of objects being dropped to the ground.

"Did you just throw that arrow at your twin?" one of the gods asked.

"Yes, I did!" said Hoder with a cheerful smile on his face. He was unaware of the terrible thing that had happened. "I'm sure Balder wasn't expecting that."

"So you don't deny it?" asked Balder's wife, the goddess Nanna.

"Of course not," said Hoder. "I threw it. . . ." Then he realized that there had been great distress in Nanna's voice. "Why? What's the matter?"

"The matter is that Balder is dead, and the arrow that killed him was thrown by you," said Thor sadly.

Horrified, Hoder explained what had happened. "I wanted to join in . . . and Loki gave me the arrow and helped me to aim, that's all. I didn't mean. . . ." His voice trailed off into silence.

At the mention of his name, a group of gods grabbed Loki, who was quietly trying to leave the scene of his dreadful crime.

"Friend or no friend, I should kill you where you stand, Loki," said Thor, blocking his path. "But Gladsheim is a place of peace, so there'll be no more killing here today."

The gods loosened their grip on Loki, who pulled himself free. He knew that he had gone too far and that there was no going back. None of the gods would forgive him for what he had done.

Loki turned and left Gladsheim for the last time, knowing that life would never be the same again.

While Nanna wept over the body of her dead husband, the mistletoe arrow still piercing his heart, the other gods hung their heads in sadness, for the law was clear.

Although they knew that Hoder had been tricked by Loki, it was Hoder's hand that had thrown the weapon that had killed the god of sunshine and happiness. By the law of the gods, this meant that Hoder would have to be punished, and the punishment was death.

Death did come to Hoder. Some time later Odin had another child, Vali. The mother of this boy was Rind, a cold goddess of the frozen earth. According to the prophecy, Vali would avenge Balder's death.

From the moment he was born, Vali began to grow before his mother's eyes. She and her nursemaid looked on in horror as the helpless baby grew into a fierce warrior in a matter of minutes. This was the man whose one mission in life was to fulfill the prophecy.

On the night he was born, Vali went to Asgard, the home of his father. There he killed his half brother Hoder, who had been tricked by Loki into killing his own twin brother. And the weapon Vali used? A single arrow. Some say that it was made from a stem of mistletoe.

But what of Loki? For those of you who think he escaped lightly while the innocent Balder died, or those of you who wonder what Frigga did on hearing of the death of her favorite child, be patient, for there is more to come. . . .

BALDER'S FATE
& LOKI'S DOWNFALL

Balder's body lay on the huge longboat, Ringhorn, and his fine possessions were laid out around him for the journey to the next life. At the edge of the water stood the gods, with Odin at the head, his two ravens, Hugin and Munin, on his shoulders, and his blue cloak billowing in the breeze.

NEXT TO ODIN stood his Valkyries, the beautiful women who took warriors who die in battle to the glorious place called Valhalla. Because he had died through Loki's trickery, Balder was denied a magnificent afterlife. He would begin his next life in Hel, where those who die of disease, accident, or old age go —a place without honor.

Thor paced up and down the shore, uneasy about the rows of giants who stood nearby as a mark of respect for the dead god. Among these giants were King Utgard-Loki, who had tricked Thor in the past, and Frey's wife, Gerda.

Odin stepped forward, removed his magic ring, Draupnir, from his arm and placed it in the ship. On that day it gained a new power: every ninth night it shed eight gold tears for the loss of Odin's favorite son, which became eight gold rings, each the size and weight of the original.

Then the giantess Hyrrokkin arrived on the back of an enormous wolf, using a pair of writhing vipers as reins. As she climbed off her mount, she asked someone to hold it.

Four warriors in bearskin shirts rushed forward. These were berserks, fearless and brutal fighters who attacked one another or rocks and trees if there was nothing else to fight.

But they couldn't control Hyrrokkin's wolf, so she had to calm him.

The giantess pushed Ringhorn down into the water. The funeral ship was so heavy and the splash so loud that it was heard in all nine worlds, including Niflheim. There Hel, Loki's hideous daughter, heard the sound and realized that Balder—killed by her father's trickery— was on his way to her.

Before the vessel drifted into the twilight, Thor stepped aboard. He held up his hammer to the sky and shouted the words that made sure that Balder's journey would be a safe one.

Then he brought the hammer down and touched it to the funeral pyre of dry wood on which the body lay. There was a shower of sparks. Flames began to lick at the dead body and soon became a sheet of roaring orange. On this, the saddest day in the history of Asgard, Balder's wife, Nanna, was overcome with grief and died. Her body was added to the pyre.

Even as Balder's corpse headed for Hel, the goddess Frigga hoped that she might be able to save her favorite son. She had asked for a volunteer to journey to Niflheim and beg the dreadful Hel to grant the one wish that only she could: to return Balder to the land of the living.

It was Hermod, messenger of the gods, who accepted this task. To speed his journey, he rode Odin's eight-legged horse, Sleipnir. He had to cross Gioll, the River of the Dead, over a bridge called Giollar—a bridge that, until that moment, had never been used by anyone living.

On the other side Hermod reached the entrance to Niflheim, where he was stopped by the hideous gatekeeper, Modgurd.

"Yesterday a whole army of dead rode over that bridge, and they didn't make as much noise as you!" she said. "Which suggests that you are very much alive and have no business here. What do you want?"

"I have come to speak to Hel," he explained. "To plead with her to return Balder and Nanna to the land of the living."

"Then you must hurry," said Modgurd. "They are already with Hel."

Hermod rode on at full speed and reached Hel's vast dining hall where he found Balder and Nanna. They were seated at a huge table.

"All over the nine worlds, everyone is grieving over the death of Balder," he told Hel. "He was loved by all. Isn't it right that you should give him back his life?"

"I am not so sure that the worlds grieve quite as much as you claim," said Hel, her rotting body hidden beneath her cloak. "If you can make everything, everywhere, living or dead, weep for the death of Balder, then I will let them both go. Otherwise they stay."

That was the message Hermod took back to Asgard, along with Odin's ring, Draupnir, which his dead son wanted returned to him. On hearing the news, Frigga sent messages to all corners of the worlds to tell all things that they must grieve the loss of her favorite child.

Soon the sound of sobbing filled the air. The grass wept dew. The rocks wept stalactites. The snow wept icicles. Tears of sap poured down the trunks of the trees.

Even Hel shed a tear in the knowledge that her father had caused Balder's death and would suffer for it. Everyone cried.

Everyone, that is, except for a giantess called Thok. When one of Frigga's messengers found her and told her of his mission, she said: "The old one's favorite boy never did much good when he was alive. I won't grieve for him. Let him stay with Hel where he belongs."

When this news reached Hel, any chance of her releasing Balder was lost. What was worse, this unkind giantess turned out not to be a giantess at all. Thok was none other than Loki in disguise.

Not content with having tricked blind Hoder into killing his twin brother, Loki was denying Balder his life a second time. No wonder that Loki fled to Midgard, the world of humans, to hide from the gods. He built a house on top of a mountain. It had a doorway in each wall, so he could see in all directions and escape if he saw someone coming.

Loki chose a place near a waterfall and spent much of the time disguised as a salmon hiding in the river beneath it.

Soon he began to worry that one day Odin might be sitting on his throne, Hlidskialf, and see him turn into a salmon, thus learning his trick. In those days people caught fish with their hands, a hook, or a spear . . . but Loki remembered the net he'd used to capture Andvari— the one the goddess Ran used to capture drowning sailors. What if one of the gods sent to hunt him down had such a net?

Loki decided to be prepared. He would make his own net, turn himself back into a salmon, and practice escaping from it. That way, if the day came when he was faced with Ran's net, he would know all the tricks. He hurried to his house, found some strong twine, sat down in front of the fire, and began to knot it into a net.

As it happened, that very morning Odin had been sitting on his throne, looking out into the nine worlds, when his eye had been drawn to Midgard and to a strange-looking house . . . with Loki inside.

Odin leaped to his feet and summoned Thor for his strength and Kvasir for his wisdom. Together they would hunt down Loki and put an end to his treachery forever.

As Loki sat in his house working on his net, he saw through an open doorway that the three gods were approaching. The moment he saw them, he threw the half-made net into the fire, then dashed out through a doorway on the other side of the house.

He almost threw himself down the mountain, his feet barely touching the rocky path as he raced to the waterfall. There he dived into the icy water, turning himself into a salmon and hiding behind a rock on the riverbed.

When the three gods entered the house, Loki was long gone, but wise Kvasir strode straight over to the hearth. The fire had been lit some time before, but someone had recently thrown something on it. He stamped out the flames and pulled the object out of the ashes.

"This looks very much like part of the goddess Ran's net," he told the others with a puzzled frown.

"But Ran would never come onto dry land, and she would never light a fire," Odin mused. "How strange."

"Enough of this," snorted Thor impatiently. "Where is Loki?"

"Nearby, I suspect," said Kvasir. "This piece of net was thrown onto the fire only recently, and look. . . ." He bent and picked up the ball of twine. "That's all this ever was, a piece of net, not a whole one."

"What would Loki want with a net?" Thor roared. He didn't want to stand there reasoning; he wanted to find Loki and put an end to him.

"That's it!" said Kvasir, suddenly. "Loki must have been testing his defenses against whatever we throw at him."

"And why would we throw a net at him?" asked Odin.

"Because he's changed himself into a fish!" said Kvasir. "As soon as he saw us coming, he must have gone to the river and changed his shape."

"The scheming shapeshifter!" muttered Thor. So the three gods set about making a fishing net with the twine Loki had left behind.

When the net was finished, the gods made their way down the mountain path, cast the net into the water, and dragged the riverbed. The net didn't quite reach the riverbed, and because Loki stayed low and behind his rock, the net came up empty.

"We must add weights to the bottom of the net," said Kvasir. "That way it will drag the riverbed and force out anyone hiding there!"

So they tied weights to the net and dragged the river a second time. At the last possible moment, Loki jumped out of the water, over the net, and up the waterfall, just as salmon do to this day.

Thor watched. He was sure that the salmon he had seen escape was none other than the slippery Loki. . . . He saw the fish fall back down the waterfall into the river. They would be ready for him next time!

For the third time Kvasir and Odin lowered the net into the water. Foolishly Loki tried using the same trick. When the net came toward him, he gave a huge jump, which carried him out of the water . . . and into the waiting arms of Thor, who caught him just above the tail.

Back in his usual form, Loki was dragged struggling into a cavern deep beneath a mountain.

"Now you will pay for your cruel tricks and the death of my twin sons!" cried Odin, his words echoing around the dark, dank walls. "I have summoned two of your children to join us."

"What do you want with them?" Loki moaned, struggling to free himself from Thor's grip.

"You shall see," said Odin grimly.

Soon two of Loki's children arrived—not Fenris the wolf, not Jormungand the giant serpent, nor Hel the goddess of death —but the two sons Loki had with his wife, the goddess Sigyn.

"They've done you no harm. Let them go!" Loki pleaded.

Odin said nothing, but simply touched the one called Vali. He instantly turned into a wolf and pounced on his brother, Narve, tearing him to shreds before his father's eyes. Odin then pulled out Narve's insides and wove them into a rope, which he, Kvasir, and Thor used to tie the struggling Loki to three huge boulders.

Odin then turned the rope into iron.

"Skadi!" he bellowed into the cavern, and a huge mountain giantess loomed out of the darkness, clutching an enormous serpent.

Without a word the giantess fixed the snake above Loki's head.

No sooner was it in place than a drop of burning poison fell from its fangs and landed on Loki's face. He screamed in agony.

"Here you will remain until the end of the world," said Odin, and—despite all the terrible things Loki had done—there was a trace of sadness in the voice of the chief of all the gods.

Thor fixed a stare upon him. "Your deeds will live on, Loki," he said. "Tales of your trickery will be told for a thousand years. . . ."

"And all that time you will be here at the mercy of the serpent's venom," Kvasir reminded him.

As the three gods turned to leave Loki, his wife, Sigyn, hurried into the cavern, clutching a large bowl, which she held above her husband's head to catch the poison from the snake's fangs.

Whenever the bowl was full, Sigyn moved it aside to tip the poison on the floor. When, in that brief moment, a drop of poison burned Loki's face, he screamed so loud and writhed in such pain that it echoed under the ground, causing earthquakes.

There Loki remains until Ragnarok—the final battle at the end of the world. Then, according to those who can read the future, Loki will be set free and will rise up with his son, the wolf Fenris, to fight alongside the giants against the gods of Asgard.

Myths and Legends Resources

Here is just a sampling of other resources to look for. These resources on myths and legends are broken down into groups. Enjoy!

General Mythology

The Children's Dictionary of Mythology *edited by David Leeming* (Franklin Watts, 1999). This volume is a dictionary of terms, names, and places in the mythology of various cultures around the world.

Creation Read-aloud Stories from Many Lands *retold by Ann Pilling* (Candlewick Press, 1997). This is a collection of sixteen stories retold in an easy style and presented in three general groups: beginnings, warmth and light, and animals.

The Crystal Pool: Myths and Legends of the World *by Geraldine McCaughrean* (Margaret K. McElderry Books, 1998). Twenty-eight myths and legends from around the world comprise this book. They include the Chinese legend "The Alchemist" and the Celtic legend "Culloch and the Big Pig."

Encyclopedia Mythica
http://www.pantheon.org/areas/mythology/
From this page of the *Encyclopedia Mythica* site you can select from any of five countries to have the mythology of that area displayed.

A Family Treasury of Myths from Around the World *retold by Viviane Koenig* (Abrams, 1998). This collection of ten stories includes myths from Egypt, Africa, Greece, and other places around the world.

Goddesses, Heroes and Shamans: The Young People's Guide to World Mythology *edited by Cynthia O'Neill and others* (Kingfisher, 1994). This book introduces the reader to over five hundred mythological characters from around the world.

Gods, Goddesses and Monsters: An Encyclopedia of World Mythology *retold by Sheila Keenan* (Scholastic, 2000). This beautifully illustrated book discusses the characters and themes of the myths of peoples from Asia to Africa, to North and South America.

The Golden Hoard: Myths and Legends of the World *retold by Geraldine McCaughrean* (Margaret K. McElderry Books, 1995). This book contains twenty-two myths and legends that are exciting, adventurous, magical, and poetic.

The Illustrated Book of Myths: Tales and Legends of the World *retold by Neil Philips* (Dorling Kindersley, 1995). This beautifully illustrated collection brings together many of the most popular of the Greek and Roman, Norse, Celtic, Egyptian, Native American, African, and Indian myths.

Kids Zone: Myths and Fables from Around the World
http://www.afroam.org/children/myths/myths.html
Just click on your choice of the sixteen stories listed, and it will appear in full text.

Legends http://www.planetozkids.com/oban/legends.htm
From this Web page you can get the full text of any of the many listings.

Mythical Birds and Beasts from Many Lands *retold by Margaret Mayo* (Dutton, 1996). This book is a collection of stories that illustrate the special powers of birds and beasts that have become a part of folklore around the world.

Mythology *by Neil Philip* (Alfred A. Knopf, 1999). This superbly illustrated volume from the "Eyewitness Books" series surveys the treatment of such topics as gods and goddesses, the heavens, creation, the elements, and evil as expressed in various mythologies around the world.

Mythology *CD-ROM for Mac and Windows* (Thomas S. Klise, 1996). Educational games and puzzles, a glossary, and a testing section are all part of this CD introduction to Greek and Roman mythology.

Myths and Legends *by Neil Philip* (DK Publishing, 1999). More than fifty myths and legends from around the world are explained through works of art, text, and annotation by one of the world's foremost experts on mythology and folklore.

The New York Public Library Amazing Mythology: A Book of Answers for Kids by *Brendan January* (John Wiley, 2000). Over two hundred questions and answers introduce myths from many ancient cultures, including Egyptian, Greek, Roman, Celtic, Norse, and Native American.

Plays from Mythology: Grades 4-6 by *L.E. McCullough* (Smith and Kraus, 1998). Twelve original plays are included, each with suggestions for staging and costumes.

Sources for Mythology
http://www.best.com/~atta/mythsrcs.html
In addition to defining mythology and distinguishing it from legend and folklore, this Web site lists primary sources for myths from many regions of the world, as well as magazines, dictionaries, and other resources relating to mythology.

Sun, Moon and Stars *retold by Mary Hoffman* (Dutton, 1998). More than twenty myths and legends from around the world, all explaining what was seen in the sky, make up this exquisitely illustrated book.

AFRICAN

African Gods and their Associates
http://www3.sympatico.ca/untangle/africang.html
This Web page gives you a list of the African gods with links to further information about them.

African Myths
http://www.cybercomm.net/~grandpa/africanmyths.html
Full text of several tales from the Kenya, Hausa, Ashanti, and Nyanja tribes are included in this Web site.

Anansi and the Talking Melon *retold by Eric A. Kimmel* (Holiday House, 1994). Anansi, a legendary character from Africa, tricks Elephant and some other animals into thinking that the melon in which he is hiding can talk.

Children's Stories from Africa 4 *Video recordings (VHS)* (Monterey Home Video, 1997). Among the African Legends on this page: "How the Hare Got His Long Legs," "How the Porcupine Got His Quills," "The Brave Sititunga," and "The Greedy Spider."

The Hero with an African Face: Mythic Wisdom of Traditional Africa by *Clyde W. Ford* (Bantam, 2000). "The Hero with an African Face" is only one of the several stories included in this book, which also includes a map of the peoples and myths of Africa and a pronunciation guide for African words.

Kings, Gods and Spirits from African Mythology *retold by Jan Knappert* (Peter Bedrick Books, 1993). This illustrated collection contains myths and legends of the peoples of Africa.

Legends of Africa by *Mwizenge Tembo* (Metro Books, 1996). This indexed and illustrated volume is from the "Myths of the World" series.

Myths and Legends *retold by O. B. Duane* (Brockhampton Press, 1998). Duane has vividly retold some of the most gripping African tales.

CELTIC

Celtic Myths *retold by Sam McBratney* (Peter Bedrick, 1997). This collection of fifteen illustrated stories draws from English, Irish, Scottish, and Welsh folklore.

Excalibur *retold by Hudson Talbott* (Books of Wonder, 1996). In this illustrated story from the legends of King Arthur, Arthur receives his magical sword, Excalibur

Irish Fairy Tales and Legends *retold by Una Leavy* (Robert Rinehart, 1996). Cuchulainn, Deirdre, and Fionn Mac Cumhail are only three of the legendary characters you will meet in this volume.

Irish Myths and Legends
http://www.mc.maricopa.edu/users/shoemaker/
    Celtic/index.html
This Web site is for those more serious in their study of Irish myths and legends.

King Arthur by *Rosalind Kerven* (DK Publishing, 1998). This book from the "Eyewitness Classic" series is a retelling of the boy who was fated to be the "Once and Future King" It includes illustrated notes to explain the historical background of the story.

Robin Hood and His Merry Men *retold by Jane Louise Curry* (Margaret K. McElderry, 1994). This collection contains seven short stories of the legendary hero Robin Hood, who lived with his band of followers in Sherwood Forest.

The World of King Arthur and his Court: People, Places, Legend and Love by *Kevin Crossley-Holland* (Dutton, 1998). The author combines legend, anecdote, fact, and speculation to help answer some of the questions regarding King Arthur and his chivalrous world.

CHINESE

Asian Mythology by *Rachel Storm* (Lorenz, 2000). Included in this volume are myths and legends of China.

Chinese Culture
http://chineseculture.about.com/culture/
    chineseculture/msub82.htm
Use this Web page as a starting point for further exploration about Chinese myths and legends.

Chinese Mythology by *Anne Birrell* (Johns Hopkins, 1999). This comprehensive introduction to Chinese mythology will meet the needs of the more serious and the general reader

Chinese Myths and Legends *retold by O. B. Duane and others* (Brockhampton Press, 1998). Introductory notes by the author give further explanation of the thirty-eight stories included in this illustrated volume.

Dragons and Demons by *Stewart Ross* (Cooper Beech, 1998). Included in this collection of myths and legends from Asia are the Chinese myths "Chang Lung the Dragon" and "The Ugly Scholar."

Dragons, Gods and Spirits from Chinese Mythology *retold by Tao Tao Liu Sanders* (Peter Bedrick Books, 1994). The stories in this book include ancient myths about nature, the gods, and creation as well as religious legends.

Fa Mulan: The Story of a Woman Warrior *retold by Robert D. San Souci* (Hyperion, 1998). Artists Jean and Mou-Sien Tseng illustrate this Chinese legend of a young heroine who is courageous, selfless, and wise.

Land of the Dragon: Chinese Myth by *Tony Allan* (Time-Life, 1999). This volume from the "Myth and Mankind" series includes many of China's myths as well as examination of the myth and its historical roots.

Selected Chinese Myths and Fantasies
http://www.chinavista.com/experience/story/story.html
From this Web site and its links you will find several Chinese myths that are enjoyed by children as well as the history of Chinese mythology.

EGYPTIAN

Egyptian Gods and Goddesses by *Henry Barker* (Grosset and Dunlap, 1999). In this book designed for the young reader, religious beliefs of ancient Egypt are discussed, as well as their gods and goddesses.

Egyptian Mythology A-Z: A Young Reader's Companion by *Pat Remler* (Facts on File, 2000). Alphabetically arranged, this resource defines words relating to Egyptian mythology.

Egyptian Myths *retold by Jacqueline Morley* (Peter Bedrick Books, 1999). Legends of the pharaohs, myths about creation, and the search for the secret of all knowledge, make up this illustrated book.

The Gods and Goddesses of Ancient Egypt by *Leonard Everett Fisher* (Holiday House, 1997). This artist/writer describes thirteen of the most important Egyptian gods.

Gods and Myths of Ancient Egypt by *Mary Barnett* (Regency House, 1996). Beautiful color photographs are used to further explain the text in this summary of Egyptian mythology.

Gods and Pharaohs from Egyptian Mythology *retold by Geraldine Harris* (Peter Bedrick Books, 1992). The author gives some background information about the Ancient Egyptians and then retells more than twenty of their myths.

Myth Man's Egyptian Homework Help
http://egyptmyth.com/
Cool Facts and Fun for Kids and *Egyptian Myth* Encyclopedia are only two of the many wonderful links this page will lead you to.

Myths and Civilizations of the Ancient Egyptians by *Sarah Quie* (Peter Bedrick Books, 1998). The author intersperses Egypt's myths with a history of its civilization in this illustrated volume.

The Secret Name of Ra *retold by Anne Rowe* (Rigby Interactive Library, 1996). In this Egyptian myth, Isis tricks Ra into revealing his secret name so that she and her husband Osiris can become rulers of the earth.

Tales from Ancient Egypt *retold by George Hart* (Hoopoe Books, 1994). The seven tales in this collection include stories of animals, of Isis and Horus, of a sailor lost on a magic island, and of pharaohs and their magicians.

Who's Who in Egyptian Mythology by *Anthony S. Mercatante* (Scarecrow Press, 1995). The author has compiled a concise, easy-to-use dictionary of ancient Egyptian deities.

GREEK

Allta and the Queen: A Tale of Ancient Greece by *Priscilla Galloway* (Annick Press, 1995). This made-up story, which is based on Homer's epic poem, *The Odyssey*, reads like a novel.

Cupid and Psyche *retold by M. Charlotte Craft* (Morrow Junior Books, 1996). This classic love story from Greek mythology will appeal to young and old.

Gods and Goddesses by *John Malam* (Peter Bedrick Books, 1999). This volume is packed with information about the important gods and goddesses of ancient Greece, including Zeus, Hera, Athena, and Hades.

Greek and Roman Mythology by *Dan Nardo* (Lucent, 1998). The author examines the historical development of Greco-Roman mythology, its heroes, and its influence on the history of Western civilization.

Guide for Using D'Aulaires' Book of Greek Myths in the Classroom by *Cynthia Ross* (Teacher Created Materials, 1993). This reproducible book includes sample plans, author information, vocabulary-building ideas, cross-curricular activities, quizzes, and many ideas for extending this classic work.

Hercules by *Robert Burleigh* (Harcourt Brace, 1999). Watercolor and color pencil illustrations help to tell the story of Hercules's final labor in which he went back to the underworld and brought back the three-headed dog, Cerberus.

Medusa by *Deborah Nourse Lattimire* (Joanna Cotler Books, 2000). The author/illustrator of this book re-creates the tragedy of one of the best-known Greek myths, the tale of the beautiful Medussa whose conceit causes a curse be placed on her.

The Myths and Legends of Ancient Greece *CD-ROM for Mac and Windows* (Clearvue, 1996). This CD conveys the heroic ideals and spirit of Greek mythology as it follows ten of the best-known myths.

Mythweb http://www.mythweb.com/
This Web page provides links to Greek gods, heroes, an encyclopedia of mythology, and teacher resources.

Pegasus, the Flying Horse *retold by Jane Yolen* (Dutton, 1998). This Greek myth tells of how Bellerophon, with the help of Athena, tames the winged horse Pegasus and conquers the monstrous Chimaera.

The Race of the Golden Apples *retold by Claire Martin* (Dial, 1991). Caldecott Medal winners Leo and Diane Dillon have illustrated this myth of Atalanta, the beautiful Greek princess.

The Random House Book of Greek Myths by *Joan D. Vinge* (Random House, 1999). The author retells some of the famous Greek myths about gods, goddesses, humans, heroes, and monsters, explaining the background of the tales and why these tales have survived.

The Robber Baby: Stories from the Greek Myths *retold by Anne Rockwell* (Greenwillow Books, 1994). Anne Rockwell, a well-known name in children's literature, has put together a superbly retold collection of myths that will be enjoyed by readers of all ages.

NORSE

Beowulf by *Welwyn Wilton Katz* (Groundwood, 2000). The illustrations in this classic legend are based on the art of the Vikings.

Favorite Norse Myths *retold by Mary Pope Osborne* (Scholastic, 1996). These fourteen tales of Norse gods, goddesses, and giants are based on the oldest written sources of Norse mythology, *Prose Edda* and *Poetic Edda*.

The Giant King by *Rosalind Kerven* (NTC Publishing Group, 1998). Photos of artifacts from the Viking Age illustrate these two stories that are rooted in Norse mythology.

Gods and Heroes from Viking Mythology by *Brian Branston* (Peter Bedrick Books, 1994). This illustrated volume tells the stories of Thor, Balder, King Gylfi, and other Nordic gods and goddesses

Handbook of Norse Mythology by *John Lindow* (Ambcc, 2001). For the advanced reader, this handbook covers the tales, their literary and oral sources, includes an A-to-Z of the key mythological figures, concepts and events, and so much more.

Kids Domain Fact File
http://www.kidsdomain.co.uk/teachers/resources/
  fact_file_viking_gods_and_goddesses.html
This child-centered Web page is a dictionary of Viking gods and goddesses.

Myths and Civilization of the Vikings by *Hazel Martell* (Peter Bedrick, 1998). Each of the nine stories in this book is followed by a non-fiction spread with information about Viking society.

Norse Mythology: The Myths and Legends of the Nordic Gods *retold by Arthur Cotterell* (Lorenz Books, 2000). This encyclopedia of the Nordic peoples' myths and legends is generously illustrated with fine art paintings of the classic stories.

Odins' Family: Myths of the Vikings *retold by Neil Philip* (Orchard Books, 1996). This collection of stories of Odin, the All-father, and the other Viking gods Thor, Tyr, Frigg, and Loer is full of excitement that encompasses both tragedy and comedy.

Stolen Thunder: A Norse Myth *retold by Shirley Climo* (Houghton Mifflin, 1994). This story, beautifully illustrated by Alexander Koshkin, retells the Norse myth about the god of Thunder and the recovery of his magic hammer Mjolnir, from the Frost Giany, Thrym.

NORTH AMERICAN

Buffalo Dance: A Blackfoot Legend *retold by Nancy Can Laan* (Little, Brown and Company, 1993). This illustrated version of the Native North American legend tells of the ritual performed before the buffalo hunt.

The Favorite Uncle Remus *by Joel Chandler Harris* (Houghton Mifflin, 1948). This classic work of literature is a collection of stories about Brer Rabbit, Brer Fox, Brer Tarrypin, and others that were told to the author as he grew up in the South.

Iktomi Loses his Eyes: A Plains Indian Story *retold by Paul Goble* (Orchard Books, 1999). The legendary character Iktomi finds himself in a predicament after losing his eyes when he misuses a magical trick.

The Legend of John Henry *retold by Terry Small* (Doubleday, 1994). This African American legendary character, a steel driver on the railroad, pits his strength and speed against the new steam engine hammer that is putting men out of jobs.

The Legend of the White Buffalo Woman *retold by Paul Goble* (National Geographic Society, 1998). This Native American Plains legend tells the story of the White Buffalo Woman who gave her people the Sacred Calf Pipe so that people would pray and commune with the Great Spirit.

Myths and Legends for American Indian Youth http://www.kstrom.net/isk/stories/myths.html Stories from Native Americans across the United States are included in these pages.

Snail Girl Brings Water: a Navajo Story *retold by Geri Keams* (Rising Moon, 1998). This retelling of a traditional Navajo re-creation myth explains how water came to earth.

The Woman Who Fell from the Sky: The Iroquois Story of Creation *retold by John Bierhirst* (William Morrow, 1993). This myth describes how the creation of the world was begun by a woman who fell down to earth from the sky country, and how it was finished by her two sons.

SOUTH AMERICAN (INCLUDING CENTRAL AMERICAN)

Gods and Goddesses of the Ancient Maya *by Leonard Everett Fisher* (Holiday House, 1999). With text and illustration inspired by the art, glyphs, and sculpture of the ancient Maya, this artist and author describes twelve of the most important Maya gods.

How Music Came to the World: An Ancient Mexican Myth *retold by Hal Ober* (Houghton Mifflin, 1994). This illustrated book, which includes author notes and a pronunciation guide, is an Aztec pourquoi story that explains how music came to the world.

Llama and the Great Flood *retold by Ellen Alexander* (Thomas Y. Crowell, 1989). In this illustrated retelling of the Peruvian myth about the Great Flood, a llama warns his master of the coming destruction and leads him and his family to refuge on a high peak in the Andes.

The Legend of the Poinsettia *retold by Tomie dePaola* (G. P. Putnam's Sons,1994). This beautifully illustrated Mexican legend tells of how the poinsettia came to be when a young girl offered her gift to the Christ child.

Lost Realms of Gold: South American Myth *edited by Tony Allan* (Time-Life Books, 2000). This volume, which captures the South American mythmakers' fascination with magic, includes the tale of the first Inca who built the city of Cuzco, as well as the story of the sky people who discovered the rain forest.

People of Corn: A Mayan Story *retold by Mary-Joan Gerson* (Little, Brown, 1995). In this richly illustrated creation story, the gods first try and fail, then try and fail again before they finally succeed.

Tales from the Rain Forest: Myths and Legends from the Amazonian Indians of Brazil *retold by Mercedes Dorson* (Ecco Press, 1997). Ten stories from this region include "The Origin of Rain" and "How the Stars Came to Be."

WHO'S WHO IN MYTHS AND LEGENDS

This is a cumulative listing of some important characters found in all eight volumes of the **World Book Myths and Legends** series.

A

Aegir (EE jihr), also called Hler, was the god of the sea and the husband of Ran in Norse myths. He was lord of the undersea world where drowned sailors spent their days.

Amma (ahm mah) was the creator of the world in the myths of the Dogon people of Africa. Mother Earth was his wife, and Water and Light were his children. Amma also created the people of the world.

Amun (AH muhn), later Amun-Ra, became the king of gods in later Egyptian myths. Still later he was seen as another form of Ra.

Anubis (uh NOO bihs) in ancient Egypt was the god of the dead and helper to Osiris. He had the head of a jackal.

Ao (ow) was a giant turtle in a Chinese myth. He saved the life of Kui.

Aphrodite (af ruh DY tee) in ancient Greece was the goddess of love. She was known for her beauty. The Romans called her Venus.

Arianrod (air YAN rohd) in Welsh legends was the mother of the hero Llew.

Arthur (AHR thur) in ancient Britain was the king of the Britons. He probably was a real person who ruled long before the age of knights in armor. His queen was Guinevere.

Athena (uh THEE nuh) in ancient Greece was the goddess of war. The Romans called her Minerva.

Atum (AH tuhm) was the creator god of ancient Egypt and the father of Shu and Tefnut. He later became Ra-Atum.

B

Babe (bayb) in North American myths was the big blue ox owned by Paul Bunyan.

Balder (BAWL dur) was the god of light in Norse myths. He was the most handsome of all gods and was Frigga's favorite son.

Balor (BAL awr) was an ancient chieftain in Celtic myths who had an evil eye. He fought Lug, the High King of Ireland.

Ban Hu (bahn hoo) was the dog god in a myth that tells how the Year of the Dog in the Chinese calendar got its name.

Bastet (BAS teht), sometimes Bast (bast) in ancient Egypt was the mother goddess. She was often shown as a cat. Bastet was the daughter of Ra and the sister of Hathor and Sekhmet.

Bellerophon (buh LEHR uh fahn) in ancient Greek myths was a hero who captured and rode the winged horse, Pegasus.

Blodeuwedd was the wife of Llew in Welsh legends. She was made of flowers woven together by magic.

Botoque (boh toh kay) in Kayapó myths was the boy who first ate cooked meat and told people about fire.

Brer Rabbit (brair RAB iht) was a clever trickster rabbit in North American myths.

C

Chameleon (kuh MEEL yuhn) in a Yoruba myth of Africa was a messenger sent to trick the god Olokun and teach him a lesson.

Conchobar (KAHN koh bahr), also called Conor, was the king of Ulster. He was a villain in many Irish myths.

Coyote (ky OH tee) was an evil god in myths of the Maidu and some other Native American people.

Crow (kroh) in Inuit myths was the wise bird who brought daylight to the Inuit people.

Cuchulain (koo KUHL ihn), also Cuchullain or Cuchulan, in Irish myths was Ireland's greatest warrior of all time. He was the son of Lug and Dechtire.

Culan (KOO luhn) in Irish myths was a blacksmith. His hound was killed by Setanta, who later became Cuchulain.

D

Davy Crockett (DAY vee KRAHK iht) was a real person. He is remembered as an American frontier hero who died in battle and also in legends as a great hunter and woodsman.

Dechtire (DEHK teer) in Irish myths was the sister of King Conchobar and mother of Cuchulain.

Deirdre (DAIR dray) in Irish myths was the daughter of Fedlimid. She refused to wed Conchobar. It was said that she would lead to Ireland's ruin.

Di Jun (dee joon) was god of the Eastern Sky in Chinese myths. He lived in a giant mulberry tree.

Di Zang Wang (dee zahng wahng) in Chinese myths was a Buddhist monk who was given that name when he became the lord of the underworld. His helper was Yan Wang, god of the dead.

Dionysus (dy uh NY suhs) was the god of wine in ancient Greek myths. He carried a staff wrapped in vines.

Dolapo was the wife of Kigbo in a Yoruba myth of Africa.

E

Eight Immortals (ihm MAWR tuhlz) in Chinese myths were eight ordinary human beings whose good deeds led them to truth and enlightenment. The Eight Immortals were godlike heroes. They had special powers to help people.

El Niño (ehl NEEN yoh) in Inca myths was the ruler of the wind, the weather, and the ocean and its creatures.

Emer (AYV ur) in Irish myths was the daughter of Forgal the Wily and wife of Cuchulain.

F

Fafnir (FAHV nihr) in Norse myths was a son of Hreidmar. He killed his father for his treasure, sent his brother Regin away, and turned himself into a dragon.

Frey (fray), also called Freyr, was the god of summer in Norse myths. His chariot was pulled by a huge wild boar.

Freya (FRAY uh) was the goddess of beauty and love in Norse myths. Her chariot was pulled by two large cats.

Frigga (FRIHG uh), also called Frigg, in Norse myths was the wife of Odin and mother of many gods. She was the most powerful goddess in Asgard.

Frog was an animal prince in an Alur myth of Africa. He and his brother, Lizard, competed for the right to inherit the throne of their father.

Fu Xi (foo shee) in a Chinese myth was a boy who, with his sister Nü Wa, freed the Thunder God and was rewarded. His name means Gourd Boy.

G

Gaunab was Death, who took on a human form in a Khoi myth of Africa. Tsui'goab fought with Gaunab to save his people.

Geb (gehb) in ancient Egypt was the Earth itself. All plants and trees grew from his back. He was the brother and husband of Nut and the father of the gods Osiris, Isis, Seth, and Nephthys.

Glooscap (glohs kap) was a brave and cunning god in the myths of Algonquian Native American people. He was a trickster who sometimes got tricked.

Guinevere (GWIHN uh vihr) in British and Welsh legends was King Arthur's queen, who was also loved by Sir Lancelot.

Gwydion (GWIHD ih uhn) in Welsh legends was the father of Llew and the nephew of the magician and ruler, Math.

H

Hades (HAY deez) in ancient Greece was the god of the dead. Hades was also called Pluto (PLOO toh). The Romans called him Dis.

Hairy Man was a frightening monster in African American folk tales.

Harpy (HAHRP ee) was one of the hideous winged women in Greek myths. The hero Jason and his Argonauts freed King Phineas from the harpies' power.

Hathor (HATH awr) was worshiped in the form of a cow in ancient Egypt, but she also appeared as an angry lioness. She was the daughter of Ra and the sister of Bastet and Sekhmet.

Heimdall (HAYM dahl) was the god in Norse myths who guarded the rainbow bridge joining Asgard, the home of the gods, to other worlds.

Hel (hehl), also called Hela, was the goddess of death in Norse myths. The lower half of her body was like a rotting corpse. Hel was Loki's daughter.

Helen (HEHL uhn), called Helen of Troy, was a real person in ancient Greece. According to legend, she was known as the most beautiful woman in the world. Her capture by Paris led to the Trojan War.

Heng E (huhng ay), sometimes called Chang E, was a woman in Chinese myths who became the moon goddess. She was the wife of Yi the Archer.

Hera (HEHR uh) in ancient Greece was the queen of heaven and the wife of Zeus. The Romans called her Juno.

Heracles (HEHR uh kleez) in ancient Greek myths was a hero of great strength. He was the son of Zeus. He had to complete twelve tremendous tasks in order to become one of the gods. The Romans called him Hercules.

Hermes (HUR meez) was the messenger of the gods in Greek myths. He wore winged sandals. The Romans called him Mercury.

Hoder (HOO dur) was Balder's twin brother in Norse myths. He was blind. It was said that after a mighty battle he and Balder would be born again.

Hoenir (HAY nihr), also called Honir, was a god in Norse myths. In some early myths, he is said to be Odin's brother.

Horus (HAWR uhs) in ancient Egypt was the son of Isis and Osiris. He was often shown with the head of a falcon. Horus fought Seth to rule Egypt.

Hreidmar (HRAYD mahr) was a dwarf king in Norse myths who held Odin for a huge pile of treasure. His sons were Otter, Fafnir, and Regin.

Hyrrokkin (HEER rahk kihn) in Norse myths was a terrifying female giant who rode an enormous wolf using poisonous snakes for reins.

I

Irin-Mage (eereen mah geh) in Tupinambá myths was the only person to be saved when the creator, Monan, destroyed the other humans. Irin-Mage became the ancestor of all people living today.

Isis (EYE sihs) in ancient Egypt was the goddess of fertility and a master of magic. She became the most powerful of all the gods and goddesses. She was the sister and wife of Osiris and mother of Horus.

J

Jade Emperor (jayd EHM puhr uhr) in Buddhist myths of China was the chief god in Heaven.

Jason (JAY suhn) was a hero in Greek myths. His ship was the Argo, and the men who sailed with him on his adventures were called the Argonauts.

Johnny Appleseed (AP uhl seed) was a real person, John Chapman. He is remembered in legends as the person who traveled across North America, planting apple orchards.

K

Kaboi (kah boy) was a very wise man in a Carajá myth. He helped his people find their way from their underground home to the surface of the earth.

Kewawkwuí (kay wow kwoo) were a group of powerful, frightening giants and magicians in the myths of Algonquian Native American people.

Kigbo (keeg boh) was a stubborn man in a Yoruba myth of Africa. His stubbornness got him into trouble with spirits.

Kodoyanpe (koh doh yahn pay) was a good god in the myths of the Maidu and some other Native American people. He was the brother of the evil god Coyote.

Kuang Zi Lian (kwahng dsee lee ehn) in a Taoist myth of China was a very rich, greedy farmer who was punished by one of the Eight Immortals.

Kui in Chinese myths was an ugly, brilliant scholar who became God of Examinations.

Kvasir (KVAH sihr) in Norse myths was the wisest of all the gods in Asgard.

L

Lancelot (lan suh laht) in British and Welsh legends was King Arthur's friend and greatest knight. He was secretly in love with Guinevere.

Lao Zi (low dzuh) was the man who founded the Chinese religion of Taoism. He wrote down the Taoist beliefs in a book, the *Tao Te Ching*.

Li Xuan (lee shwahn) was one of the Eight Immortals in ancient Chinese myths.

Light (lyt) was a child of Amma, the creator of the world, in a myth of the Dogon people of Africa.

Lizard (LIHZ urd) was an animal prince in an Alur myth of Africa. He was certain that he, and not his brother, Frog, would inherit the throne of their father.

Llew Llaw Gyffes (LE yoo HLA yoo GUHF ehs), also Lleu Law Gyffes, was a hero in Welsh myths who had many adventures. His mother was Arianrod and his father was Gwydion.

Loki (LOH kee) in Norse myths was a master trickster. His friends were Odin and Thor. Loki was half giant and half god, and could be funny and also cruel. He caused the death of Balder.

Lord of Heaven was the chief god in some ancient Chinese myths.

Lug (luk) in Irish myths was the Immortal High King of Ireland, Master of All Arts.

M

Maira-Monan (mah ee rah moh nahn) was the most powerful son of Irin-Mage in Tupinambá myths. He was destroyed by people who were afraid of his powers.

Manco Capac (mahn kih kah pahk) in Inca myths was the founder of the Inca people. He was one of four brothers and four sisters who led the Inca to their homeland.

Manitou (MAN ih toh) was the greatest and most powerful of all gods in Native American myths of the Iroquois people.

Math (mohth) in Welsh myths was a magician who ruled the Welsh kingdom of Gwynedd.

Michabo (mee chah boh) in the myths of Algonquian Native American people was the Great Hare, who taught people to hunt and brought them luck. He was a son of West Wind.

Monan (moh nahn) was the creator in Tupinambá myths.

Monkey (MUNG kee) is the hero of many Chinese stories. The most cunning of all monkeys, he became the king of monkeys and caused great troubles for the gods.

N

Nanook (na NOOK) was the white bear in myths of the Inuit people.

Naoise (NEE see) in Irish myths was Conchobar's nephew and the lover of Deirdre. He was the son of Usnech and brother of Ardan and Ainle.

Nekumonta (neh koo mohn tah) in Native American myths of the Iroquois people was a person whose goodness helped him save his people from a terrible sickness.

Nü Wa (nyuh wah) in a Chinese myth was a girl who, with her brother, Fu Xi, freed the Thunder God and was rewarded. Her name means Gourd Girl.

Nuada (NOO uh thuh) in Irish myths was King of the Tuatha Dé Danann, the rulers of all Ireland. He had a silver hand.

O

Odin (OH dihn), also called Woden, in Norse myths was the chief of all the gods and a brave warrior. He had only one eye. He was the husband of Frigga and father of many of the gods. His two advisers were the ravens Hugin and Munin.

Odysseus (oh DIHS ee uhs) was a Greek hero who fought in the Trojan War. The poet Homer wrote of his many adventures.

Oedipus (ED uh puhs) was a tragic hero in Greek myths. He unknowingly killed his own father and married his mother.

Olodumare (oh loh doo mah ray) was the supreme god in Yoruba myths of Africa.

Olokun (oh loh koon) was the god of water and giver of life in Yoruba myths of Africa. He challenged Olodumare for the right to rule.

Orpheus (AWR fee uhs) in Greek myths was famed for his music. He followed his wife, Euridice, to the kingdom of the dead to plead for her life.

Osiris (oh SY rihs) in ancient Egypt was the ruler of the dead in the kingdom of the West. He was the brother and husband of Isis and the father of Horus.

P

Pamola (pah moh lah) in the myths of Algonquian Native American people was an evil spirit of the night.

Pan Gu (pahn goo) in Chinese myths was the giant who was the first living being.

Pandora (pan DAWR uh) in ancient Greek myths was the first woman.

Paris (PAR ihs) was a real person, a hero from the city of Troy. He captured Helen, the queen of a Greek kingdom, and took her to Troy.

Paul Bunyan (pawl BUHN yuhn) was a tremendously strong giant lumberjack in North American myths.

Perseus (PUR see uhs) was a human hero in myths of ancient Greece. His most famous adventure was killing Medusa, a creature who turned anyone who looked at her to stone.

Poseidon (puh SY duhn) was the god of the sea in myths of ancient Greece. He carried a three-pronged spear called a trident to make storms and control the waves. The Romans called him Neptune.

Prometheus (pruh MEE thee uhs) was the cleverest of the gods in Greek myths. He was a friend to humankind.

Q

Queen Mother of the West was a goddess in Chinese myths.

R

Ra (rah), sometimes Re (ray), was the sun god of ancient Egypt. He was often shown with the head of a hawk. Re became the most important god. Other gods were sometimes combined with him and had Ra added to their names.

Ran (rahn) was the goddess of the sea in Norse myths. She pulled sailors from their boats in a large net and dragged them underwater.

Red Jacket in Chinese myths was an assistant to Wen Chang, the god of literature. His job was to help students who hadn't worked very hard.

S

Sekhmet (SEHK meht) in ancient Egypt was a blood-thirsty goddess with the head of a lioness. She was the daughter of Ra and the sister of Bastet and Hathor.

Setanta in Irish myths was Cuchulain's name before he killed the hound of Culan.

Seth (set), sometimes Set, in ancient Egypt was the god of chaos and confusion, who fought Horus to rule Egypt. He was the evil son of Geb and Nut.

Shanewis (shah nay wihs) in Native American myths of the Iroquois people was the wife of Nekumonta.

Shu (shoo) in ancient Egypt was the father of the sky goddess Nut. He held Nut above Geb, the Earth, to keep the two apart.

Sinchi Roca was the second emperor of the Inca. According to legend, he was the son of Ayar Manco (later known as Manco Capac) and his sister Mama Ocllo.

Skirnir (SKEER nihr) in Norse myths was a brave, faithful servant of the god Frey.

Sphinx (sfihngks) in Greek myths was a creature that was half lion and half woman, with eagle wings. It killed anyone who failed to answer its riddle.

T

Tefnut (TEHF noot) was the moon goddess in ancient Egypt. She was the sister and wife of Shu and the mother of Nut and Geb.

Theseus (THEE see uhs) was a human hero in myths of ancient Greece. He killed the Minotaur, a half-human, half-bull creature, and freed its victims.

Thor (thawr) was the god of thunder in Norse myths. He crossed the skies in a chariot pulled by goats and had a hammer, Mjollnir, and a belt, Meginjardir.

Thunder God (THUN dur gahd) in Chinese myths was the god of thunder and rain. He got his power from water and was powerless if he could not drink.

Tsui'goab (tsoo ee goh ahb) was the god of rain in myths of the Khoi people of Africa. He was a human who became a god after he fought to save his people.

Tupan (too pahn) was the spirit of thunder and lightning in Inca myths.

Tyr (tihr) was the god of war in Norse myths. He was the bravest god and was honorable and true, as well. He had just one hand.

U

Utgard-Loki (OOT gahrd LOH kee) in Norse myths was the clever, crafty giant king of Utgard. He once disguised himself as a giant called Skrymir to teach Thor a lesson.

W

Water God (WAW tur gahd) in Chinese myths was a god who sent rain and caused floods.

Wen Chang (wehn chuhng) in Chinese myths was the god of literature. His assistants were Kui and Red Jacket.

Wu (woo) was a lowly courtier in a Chinese myth who fell in love with a princess.

X

Xi He (shee heh) in Chinese myths was the goddess wife of Di Jun, the god of the eastern sky.

Xiwangmu (shee wahng moo) in Chinese myths was the owner of the Garden of Immortal Peaches.

Xuan Zang (shwahn dsahng), also called Tripitaka, was a real person, a Chinese Buddhist monk who traveled to India to gather copies of religious writings. Legends about him tell that Monkey was his traveling companion.

Y

Yan Wang (yahn wahng) was the god of the dead and judge of the first court of the Underworld in Chinese myths. He was helper to Di Zang Wang.

Yao (yow) was a virtuous emperor in Chinese myths. Because Yao lived simply and was a good leader, Yi the Archer was sent to help him.

Yi (yee) was an archer in Chinese myths who was sent by Di Jun to save the earth, in answer to Yao's prayers.

Z

Zeus (zoos) in ancient Greece was the king of gods and the god of thunder and lightning. The Romans called him Jupiter.

Zhao Shen Xiao (zhow shehn shi ow) in Chinese myths was a good magistrate, or official, who arrested the greedy merchant Kuang Zi Lian.

MYTHS AND LEGENDS GLOSSARY

This is a cumulative glossary of some important places and terms found in all eight volumes of the **World Book Myths and Legends** series.

A

Alfheim (AHLF hym) in Norse myth was the home of the light elves.

Asgard (AS gahrd) in Norse myths was the home of the warrior gods who were called the Aesir. It was connected to the earth by a rainbow bridge.

Augean (aw JEE uhn) stables were stables that the Greek hero Heracles had to clean as one of his twelve labors. He made the waters of two rivers flow through the stables and wash away the filth.

Avalon (AV uh lahn) in British legends was the island where King Arthur was carried after he died in battle. The legend says he will rise again to lead Britain.

B

Bard (bahrd) was a Celtic poet and singer in ancient times. A bard entertained people by making up and singing poems about brave deeds.

Battle of the Alamo (AL uh moh) was a battle between Texas settlers and Mexican forces when Texas was fighting for independence from Mexico. It took place at the Alamo, a fort in San Antonio, in 1836.

Bifrost (BEE fruhst) in Norse myths was a rainbow bridge that connected Asgard with the world of people.

Black Land in ancient Egypt was the area of fertile soil around the banks of the River Nile. Most people lived there.

Brer Rabbit (brair RAB iht) myths are African American stories about a rabbit who played tricks on his friends. The stories grew out of animal myths from Africa.

C

Canoe Mountain in a Maidu myth of North America was the mountain on which the evil Coyote took refuge from a flood sent to drown him.

Changeling (CHAYNG lihng) in Celtic myths was a fairy child who had been swapped with a human baby at birth. Changelings were usually lazy and clumsy.

Confucianism (kuhn FYOO shuhn IHZ uhm) is a Chinese way of life and religion. It is based on the teachings of Confucius, also known as Kong Fu Zi, and is more than 2,000 years old.

Creation myths (kree AY shuhn mihths) are myths that tell how the world began.

D

Dwarfs (dwawrfs) in Norse myths were small people of great power. They were skilled at making tools and weapons.

F

Fairies (FAIR eez) in Celtic myths were called the Little People. They are especially common in Irish legends, where they are called leprechauns.

Fomors (FOH wawrz) in Irish myths were hideous giants who invaded Ireland and were fought by Lug.

G

Giants (JY uhnts) in Norse myths were huge people who had great strength and great powers. They often struggled with the warrior gods of Asgard.

Gnome (nohm) was a small, odd-looking person in the myths of many civilizations. In Inca myths, for example, gnomes were tiny people with very big beards.

Golden Apples of the Hesperides (heh SPEHR uh deez) were apples of gold in a garden that only the Greek gods could enter. They were collected by the hero Heracles as one of his twelve labors.

Golden fleece was the fleece of a ram that the Greek hero Jason won after many adventures with his ship, Argo, and his companion sailors, the Argonauts.

Green Knoll (nohl) was the home of the Little People, or fairies, in Irish and Scottish myths.

J

Jotunheim (YUR toon hym) in Norse myths was the land of the giants.

L

Lion men in myths of Africa were humans who can turn themselves into lions.

Little People in Celtic legends and folk tales are fairies. They are often fine sword makers and blacksmiths.

M

Machu Picchu (MAH choo PEE choo) is the ruins of an ancient city built by the Inca in the Andes Mountains of Peru.

Medecolin (may day coh leen) were a tribe of evil sorcerers in the myths of Algonquian Native American people.

Medicine (MEHD uh sihn) **man** is a wise man or shaman who has special powers. Medicine men also appear as beings with special powers in myths of Africa and North and South America. Also see **Shaman.**

Midgard (MIHD gahrd) in Norse myths was the world of people.

Muspell (MOOS pehl) in Norse myths was part of the Underworld. It was a place of fire.

N

Nidavellir in Norse myths was the land of the dwarfs.

Niflheim in Norse myths was part of the Underworld. It included Hel, the kingdom of the dead.

Nirvana (nur VAH nuh) in the religion of Buddhism is a state of happiness that people find when they have freed themselves from wanting things. People who reach Nirvana no longer have to be reborn.

O

Oracle (AWRR uh kuhl) in ancient Greece was a sacred place served by people who could foretell the future. Greeks journeyed there to ask questions about their fortunes. Also see **Soothsayer.**

P

Pacariqtambo (pahk kah ree TAHM boh) in Inca myths was a place of three caves from which the first people stepped out into the world. It is also called Paccari Tampu.

Poppykettle was a clay kettle made for brewing poppy-seed tea. In an Inca myth, a poppykettle was used for a boat.

Prophecy (PRAH feh see) is a prediction made by someone who foretells the future.

R

Ragnarok (RAHG nah ruhk) in Norse myths was the final battle of good and evil, in which the giants would fight against the gods of Asgard.

S

Sahara (sah HAH rah) is a vast desert that covers much of northern Africa.

Seriema was a bird in a Carajá myth of South America whose call led the first people to try to find their way from underground to the surface of the earth.

Shaman (SHAH muhn) can be a real person, a medicine man or wise person who knows the secrets of nature. Shamans also appear as beings with special powers in some myths of North and South America. Also see **Medicine man.**

Soothsayer (sooth SAY ur) in ancient Greece was someone who could see into the future. Also see **Oracle.**

Svartalfheim (SVAHRT uhl hym) in Norse myths was the home of the dark elves.

T

Tar Baby was a sticky doll made of tar used to trap Brer Rabbit, a tricky rabbit in African American folk tales.

Tara (TAH rah) in Irish myths was the high seat, or ruling place, of the Irish kings.

Trickster (TRIHK stur) **animals** are clever ones that appear in many myths of North America, South America, and Africa.

Trojan horse. See **Wooden horse of Troy.**

Tuatha dÈ Danann (THOO uh huh day DUH nuhn) were the people of the goddess Danu. Later they were known as gods of Ireland themselves.

V

Vanaheim (VAH nah hym) in Norse myths was the home of the fertility gods.

W

Wadjet eye was a symbol used by the people of ancient Egypt. It stood for the eye of the gods Ra and Horus and was supposed to bring luck.

Wheel of Transmigration (tranz my GRAY shuhn) in the religion of Buddhism is the wheel people's souls reach after they die. From there they are sent back to earth to be born into a higher or lower life.

Wooden horse of Troy was a giant wooden horse built by the Greeks during the Trojan War. The Greeks hid soldiers in the horse's belly and left the horse for the Trojans to find.

Y

Yang (yang) is the male quality of light, sun, heat, and dryness in Chinese beliefs. Yang struggles with Yin for control of things.

Yatkot was a magical tree in an African myth of the Alur people.

Yggdrasil (IHG drah sihl) in Norse myths was a mighty tree that held all three worlds together and reached up into the stars.

Yin (yihn) is the female quality of shadow, moon, cold, and water in Chinese beliefs. Yin struggles with Yang for control of things.

CUMULATIVE INDEX

This is an alphabetical list of important topics covered in all eight volumes of the **World Book Myths and Legends** series. Next to each entry is at least one pair of numbers separated by a slash mark (/). For example, the entry for Argentina is "**Argentina** 8/4". The first number tells you what volume to look in for information. The second number tells you what page you should turn to in that volume. Sometimes a topic appears in more than one place. When it does, additional volume and page numbers are given. Here's a reminder of the volume numbers and titles: 1, *African Myths and Legends*; 2, *Ancient Egyptian Myths and Legends*; 3, *Ancient Greek Myths and Legends*; 4, *Celtic Myths and Legends*; 5, *Chinese Myths and Legends*; 6, *Norse Myths and Legends*; 7, *North American Myths and Legends*; 8, *South American Myths and Legends*.

For information on other World Book products, visit our Web site at www.worldbook.com or call 1-800-WORLDBK (967-5325).

For information on sales to schools and libraries, call 1-800-975-3250.

Cover background illustration by Paul Perreault

World Book, Inc.
233 North Michigan Avenue
Chicago, IL 60601

Pages 1–47: format and illustrations, ©1997 Belitha Press; text, ©1997 Philip Ardagh

Printed in Hong Kong
2 3 4 5 6 7 8 9 10 10 09 08 07 06 05 04 03 02

ISBN(set): 0-7166-2613-6
African Myths and Legends
ISBN: 0-7166-2605-5
LC: 2001026492
Ancient Egyptian Myths and Legends
ISBN: 0-7166-2606-3
LC: 2001026501
Ancient Greek Myths and Legends
ISBN: 0-7166-2607-1
LC: 2001035959
Celtic Myths and Legends
ISBN: 0-7166-2608-X
LC: 2001026496
Chinese Myths and Legends
ISBN: 0-7166-2609-8
LC: 2001026489
Norse Myths and Legends
ISBN: 0-7166-2610-1
LC: 2001026488
North American Myths and Legends
ISBN: 0-7166-2611-X
LC: 2001026490
South American Myths and Legends
ISBN: 0-7166-2612-8
LC: 2001026491